SALVAGE STYLE
for the GARDEN

FOR

ROBERT T.C. MILLER, ARCHITECT

AND HIS SONS

ROBERT BENNETT MILLER

MARK CHRISTOPHER MILLER

MICHAEL DOYLE MILLER

Art Director: Dana M. Irwin

Photographer: Sandra Stambaugh

Cover Designer: Barbara Zaretsky

Illustrator: Olivier Rollin

Assistant Art Director: Hannes Charen

Assistant Editors: Veronika Alice Gunter, Rain Newcomb

Production Assistance: Lorelei Buckley, Shannon Yokeley

Location Coordinators: Jeff Hamilton, Stanley Morgan

Editorial Assistance: Delores Gosnell, Rosemary Kast

Editorial Intern: Jason McGill

Special Photography: Antique Rose Emporium, Architectural Salvage Warehouse, Grace Cathey, Henry Hine, Metrolina Antiques & Fine Collectibles Show, Minchinhampton Architectural Salvage Company, Brad Oliver Antiques, Sanoma Syndication/Hans Zeegers, James Christopher Sittig, Uniquities Architectural Antiques, David Wilgus

Library of Congress Cataloging-in-Publication Data

Miller, Marcianne.
    Salvage style for the garden : simple outdoor projects using reclaimed treasures/
    Marcianne Miller with Dana Irwin.— 1st ed.
        p. cm.
        ISBN 1-57990-370-3
        1. Garden ornaments and furniture. 2. Buildings—Salvaging. 3. Building
    materials—Recycling. I. Irwin, Dana. II. Title.

    SB473.5 .M55 2003
    717—dc21

2002040649

10 9 8 7 6 5 4 3 2 1
First Edition

Published by Lark Books, a division of
Sterling Publishing Co., Inc.
387 Park Avenue South, New York, N.Y. 10016

© 2003, Lark Books

Distributed in Canada by Sterling Publishing,
c/o Canadian Manda Group, One Atlantic Ave., Suite 105
Toronto, Ontario, Canada M6K 3E7

Distributed in the U.K. by Guild of Master Craftsman Publications
Ltd., Castle Place, 166 High Street, Lewes, East Sussex, England
BN7 1XU
Tel: (+ 44) 1273 477374, Fax: (+ 44) 1273 478606, Email:
pubs@thegmcgroup.com, Web: www.gmcpublications.com

Distributed in Australia by Capricorn Link (Australia) Pty Ltd., P.O.
Box 704, Windsor, NSW 2756 Australia

If you have questions or comments about this book, please contact:

Lark Books
67 Broadway
Asheville, NC 28801
(828) 253-0467

Printed in China

ISBN 1-57990-370-3

SALVAGE STYLE
for the GARDEN

Simple
Outdoor
Projects
Using
Reclaimed
Treasures

Marcianne Miller
with Dana Irwin

LARK BOOKS

A Division of Sterling Publishing Co., Inc.
New York

TABLE of CONTENTS

INTRODUCTION   6

BASICS   8

EASY PROJECTS

Medallion Sundial   28

New-Life Birdfeeder   30

Slender Path Arbor   31

Summer Patio Bar   32

Handsome Handle Door Knocker   34

Cool-White Pedestal Tables   36

Gallery   38

PLANTERS BIG & SMALL

Cutting Edge Copper Kettle Planters   40

Rusty Star Planter   43

Stately Tin Tile Planters   44

Gorgeous Glass Hanging Planters   46

Shutter-Slat Veneer Planters   48

Good Morning Flower Bed   50

Gallery   53

GARDEN FURNITURE

Andiron Children's Bench   54

Panel-Door Garden Bench   56

Small Garden Shelves   60

Barn Wood Adirondack Chairs   62

King-Size Scrap Yard Steel Bench   68

Window-Leg Table   70

Gallery   72

PRETTY & PRACTICAL PROJECTS

Clever Lattice-Wood Boxes   74

Sturdy Metal Edging   78

Welcome Address Post   82

Victorian Chickadee Birdhouse   84

Vintage Heat Register Doormat   89

Firewood Rack with Portholes   90

Grate Steppingstones   92

Pipe Wave Fence   95

Gallery   99

SENSATIONAL SALVAGE

Garden Goddess Trellis	104
Marvelous Mello Fountain	107
Nature Lovers Garden Shrine	111
Majestic Beadboard Columns	114
Mosaic Garden Panels	116
Special Occasion Pergola	118
Vintage Glass Window	123
Sparkling Party Mobile	127
Gallery	130

WHIMSICAL ART SALVAGE

Fancy Flying Spindles	134
Lawn Chess Set	136
Happy Garden Bird	140
Gazing Ball Scarecrow	142
Giant Pin Wheel	144
Salvage Treasures Window	147
Fantastic Flamingos & Friends	150
Gallery	155

CONTRIBUTING DESIGNERS	158
ACKNOWLEDGMENTS	160
INDEX	160

INTRODUCTION

Working with salvage materials is something that feels so *right*. It's amazing how quickly you learn to love the objects that other people have thrown away. You're energized by the challenge of their nicks and misshapen parts, fascinated by the slivers of the past they have captured. Nothing quite matches the thrill of uncovering their hidden potential and transforming them into things of beauty. Best of all, you rediscover how creative you really are when you don't have to do it perfectly.

Architectural salvage, technically, refers to any detail saved from a building—a house, church, department store, factory, or other structure that has undergone renovation or demolition. In this book you'll see projects that use such strictly "architectural" details as hardwood flooring, fireplace equipment, beadboard wall panels, safety grates, roofing tiles, window frames, porch railings, door hardware, drain pipes, even bathroom fixtures.

Since this book is about outdoor projects, it seemed natural to expand beyond building-only salvage to include many wonderful items rescued from the outdoors, such as farm and garden tools, concrete curbs, brick patios, and garden statuary. Thus, you'll see some projects in *Salvage Style for the Garden* made from objects that renovation purists might reject. On the other hand, although many of our pieces were reborn from temporary resting places in a salvage yard, they're not "junk art" either, because we only rarely used pieces from machinery and automobiles.

By their nature, salvaged objects are usually old and often weathered, as well as broken or incomplete. They

also have a beautiful patina that can't ever be manufactured—the venerable silver grey of aged wood and the unmistakable color and feel of rusty metal. Ornate objects, that show off their Victorian curlicues or Deco diagonals with unrestrained pride, have become quite popular. At the same time, more and more salvagers are falling in love with remnants of rustic simplicity and solid plainness.

An object with timeworn imperfections that make it unwelcome inside the home suddenly finds itself quite desirable in the more forgiving area just beyond the back door. There's something about being outside that brings out the joy in us. In fact, many artists who work with architectural salvage work only on outdoor projects. They love the freedom that outdoor projects give them, the opportunity to create objects that play harmony with the wind and the rain.

For many artists, salvage style gives them permission to make something big. Let's face it, making a pinwheel from salvaged metal that a child can carry in her hands is fun. But making a pinwheel that is giant enough for all the neighbors to see—that's *really* fun!

In *Salvage Style for the Garden*, our designers were charged with creating a project made with architectural salvage that was completely different from the object's original purpose. They didn't fix up an old door—they turned it into a picnic table or a patio bench. If an object was supposed to hang from a ceiling when it was first manufactured, now it might be upside down as a candleholder, or transformed into a stunning planter. Lattice wood became luminarias, heat registers turned into steppingstones, broken pieces combined with one another to become a new whole project that makes the garden sparkle.

Lovers of architectural salvage discover their passion for it through many different inspirations. "Old craftsmanship invigorates me." "I'm crazy about things with a past." "I feel good giving new life to old things." "It's unique...affordable... fun!"

Whatever moves your curiosity about architectural salvage, may you embrace it wholeheartedly. We hope you enjoy *Salvage Style for the Garden*—we had great fun bringing it to you.

Basics

Welcome to the world of making new things from old things! The pathways of this world are different from the ones you may be used to—they go toward old barns, demolition sites, flea markets, scrap yards, and long-ignored garages. Once you become familiar with architectural salvage, your definition of what is beautiful undergoes a radical shift. Rust becomes lovely. Worn and weathered is desirable. Broken means "Aha! A new part!" And the question "What in the world is that?" immediately prompts another question: "What wonderful thing can I make out of it?"

Beautiful rusty metal and weathered wood are the most popular stars of salvage style.

Salvage Style for the Garden is about combining the spontaneous aspect of salvage style art with principles of good design to create projects that you'll be proud to enjoy and show off for a long time. The projects demonstrate a wide range of salvage style projects, made from materials and objects that are relatively easy to find.

Sundial salvage style: simple, easy, sensational.

For many people, the term "architectural salvage" brings up notions of mahogany pews polished for centuries by chanting monks, or marble floor tiles from palatial mansions. Yes, that is architectural salvage and don't we wish we could afford a few specimens? More likely, though, the architectural salvage you'll work with is more recent, probably not much older than siding from a barn built at the turn of the century, or a tin ceiling from a restaurant that opened when a cup of coffee was included free with the price of the luncheon special.

Victorian chimney pots—clay, concrete, and metal—have become extremely popular in gardens on both sides of the Atlantic. They make wonderful planters and pedestals.

Paradise is an empty truck and a neatly packed emporium of architectural salvage.

We've used some antique salvage objects in the projects. Check out the Victorian chimney pot planter on the cover and the medallion in the Medallion Sundial on page 28. We've also used objects that were first made only a generation or two ago, such as the 1950s ashtray turned into a birdfeeder on page 30. Whether very old or newly old, the items were indeed salvaged and transformed from their original purpose into something very different.

Because there's such a huge range of architectural details available, artisans of almost every specialty can apply their skills to salvage style. You'll see projects for master craftspeople, including woodworking projects such as the Special Occasion Pergola on page 118, and metal welding projects such as the Fantastic Flamingos on page 150. You'll also see many projects, especially in our first section, Easy Projects, for which the only skill you need is a good eye for finding things.

Right: The most surprising salvage items, old sink pedestals for instance, can be transformed into stunning garden furniture.

Where to Find Architectural Salvage

Once you're aware of architectural salvage, an amazing thing happens—you start seeing it everywhere. Literally. Lying next to your neighbor's weekly trash. Buried in a pile of junk at a yard sale. Forgotten for decades in Uncle Leo's workshop.

After your first serendipitous discoveries, you'll quickly settle on your favorite salvage haunts, and become best friends with your local architectural salvage dealers. You'll be spending Saturday mornings roaming the neighborhood for tag sales and checking out the bargain bins at the antique shops. In quick time, you'll uncover more unusual sources. As one of our designers keeps saying, "Don't forget the dumpsters behind tile stores!"

Wonderful salvage possibilities present themselves in local "exchange" newspapers, where buyers and sellers can easily connect. And don't forget the Internet. Your budget might not warrant ordering a Gothic stone

Fancy corbels and brightly colored column capitals make fantastic garden accents.

window from England shipped to you in Montana, but isn't it fun to look at all the wonderful treasures out there waiting for some other lucky salvage artist to find? And when your truck's in the repair shop and you've got no way to go salvage hunting, the Internet takes you all over the world, showing you salvage treasures you never even knew existed.

Once you're aware of architectural salvage, an amazing thing happens——you start seeing it everywhere.

Far left: This project uses salvage pieces rescued from many sources.

Left: Salvage style treasures are often hidden under piles of newer cast-offs in neighborhood flea markets.

A BRIEF SALVAGE STYLE GLOSSARY

Balusters

Escutcheon

Beadboard

Discovering the story of one piece of architectural salvage inevitably leads to finding others. Soon you'll acquire a new vocabulary, terms that in time can lead you to learn how old a piece is, where it came from, how it was manufactured, and how it was used. Here are some terms describing objects used in Salvage Style for the Garden projects.

Muntins

Spindle

Baluster: an upright support piece for rails, tables, or chair backs, often vase-like in shape

Balustrade: a rail or row of balusters, such as from a porch railing

Beadboard: a type of wood paneling that resembles tongue-in-groove planks, known for its distinctive thin, vertical stripes

Corbel: a bracket, usually of brick, stone, or wood, that supports a cornice or arch

Cornice: a horizontal piece that crowns a building or wall, or the molding between the ceiling and the wall

Escutcheon: a protective or ornamental metal plate, such as around a keyhole or drawer pull

Finial: a crowning ornament, made of concrete, wood, metal, or terra cotta

Molding or Moulding: decorative trim, usually wood, around windows and door openings, ceilings, and floors

Muntin: a strip, usually of wood or metal, that holds panes of glass in a window

Newel: a post that supports a handrail at the top or bottom, thus it's usually quite solid

Spindle: a wood piece, turned and usually decorative, often the same as, or smaller than, a baluster

Stile: pieces of framing that separate and support panels in a door

Corbel

Finial

SALVAGE
DOLLARS

There are plenty of tales in salvage lore about that fantastic salvage piece found for free on the side of the road. The Slender Path Arbor in the photo to the right is in that category and so are some of the pieces from the Victorian Chickadee Birdhouse on page 84. Believe it or not, the cupola on the top of the fabulous gazebo on page 130 was also a found treasure.

"Salvage" isn't a synonym for "free." More often than not, you'll pay for the salvage materials you want. Deconstructing old buildings and rescuing architectural

What a luxury to see salvage items, such as old cast iron pillar caps and chimney pots, displayed in such a user-friendly manner.

salvage is hard work and can be dangerous, too. So it's not unreasonable for salvage professionals to want a profit for their labor. This doesn't mean you can't haggle about prices, it just means to be aware of how much effort and expertise was invested in bringing a special salvaged piece into your hands.

The more pristine a piece is, the more other people want it, and thus the more costly it will be. If you dream

Sometimes dreams do come true—a beautiful salvage style project for free.

Sometimes you come upon a piece of salvage that is so fantastic—old, attractive, and affordable—that you can't take your eyes off it. But you haven't the foggiest idea what to do with it. Should you buy it? If you've got so much salvage in your backyard that even your dogs want to leave home, then the answer is "no." If you do indeed finish most of the things you start, go ahead and get it. Don't worry about what to do with it. The piece will eventually tell you.

The question becomes an even more wrenching issue when you find yourself presented with the opportunity to acquire salvage objects in multiples. One big blue bottle is a beautiful decorator accent in your windowsill—

Above: This rare old window with swag muntins and a hand-carved center is something a collector might buy and a salvage artist would contemplate for inspiration.

of hanging a vintage stained glass panel from your porch, know you'll pay dear for it. Salvaging perfect pieces is more the hobby of the collector than the salvage artist. The salvage artist finds a serviceable old window frame that needs work, some clear old wavy glass panes, adds a piece of broken stained glass, and creates something totally "new." Look at the Vintage Glass Window project on page 124 to see what we mean.

Remember that geography affects the availability of salvage objects, as well as the price you'll pay for them. You're likely to find reasonably priced farm-related items, for example, in an area that still has some working farms. Heavy Spanish-style mantelpieces are easier to find in the American Southwest than outside Cleveland, Ohio. It's rare to find American salvage objects in Europe, though you can find European pieces throughout the United States and Canada.

Right: Old barn wood is still available in rural and semi-rural areas.

would a hundred of them become the landscape edging you've been dreaming about for months? A few of those old railroad spikes would look fantastic turned into charming metal flowers—would having several dozen be the push you need to start making your designs for resale? Do you have the space to store multiple objects until you can use them? Or will they move from one unused pile to another? Assessing your approach to salvage style early in the process will help you all the way down the line of your creativity.

SALVAGE BUDDIES

If you're a serious hunter of valuable antiques and you don't want anyone else to grab the once-in-a-lifetime bargains, salvaging for you is probably a solitary pursuit.

Create dramatic displays by using multiples of similar objects.

Far left: It's hard to resist buying multiples when you find treasures such as this antique edging.

Far right: Two salvage buddies with very different skills collaborated on this beautiful patio bar.

SKILLS NEEDED FOR SALVAGE STYLE PROJECTS

If the last craft project you tried was a paint-by-number poodle you found in Aunt Edna's attic, can you really make salvage style projects for your garden? You surely can! Most of the projects in this book are well within the home maintenance skills of the average person.

For most people, though, salvage style treasure hunting is usually done most effectively with a buddy. One person knows wood, the other knows metal. One finds things, the other one lugs them home. One is a compulsive buyer, the other shouts "Whoa!" You get the idea.

Salvage hunting buddies seem to be a cheerier lot than other bargain hunters. They might both spy the same beautiful object, but instead of fighting over it, salvage lovers typically compete with one another to come up with what would be the best way to transform it. If you don't already have a salvage buddy, go it alone for a while. Frequent the popular salvage haunts, and before you know it, you'll be planning salvage hunting runs with a new friend.

General crafters will also find many suitable projects that will expand the horizon of their skills. The beauty of outdoor salvage style projects is that they don't have to be perfect to be functional and beautiful. If you appreciate vintage things and are open to the satisfaction of imperfection, you'll be very pleased with all the projects in the book.

A few projects—we are dreamers of course—are presented as challenges and sources of inspiration. Yet, even those projects are within your grasp. Here's why: Salvage projects really have two phases of creation. The first phase is finding the salvaged objects and imagining what they can become. Anyone who likes to rummage around in old buildings and attics can do that. The second phase is actually making the project. If you don't want to or don't have the skills yet to make the project yourself, you'll learn enough from the project instructions to take your salvage pieces and your ideas to someone who does know how to put them all together.

SALVAGE STYLE MATERIALS AND TOOLS

Far left: It was easy turning an ashtray into a birdfeeder.

Common sense tells you what tools you'll need to get started on salvage style projects. Unless you just moved into your first home, it's pretty likely that you already have most of the basic tools you'll need: hammer, nails, pliers, screwdrivers, a power drill and bits, all-purpose adhesive, tape measure, wire cutters, handsaw, chisel, and putty knife. If you need more tools, don't worry too much. You can borrow them from a more experienced salvage buddy. Or, as often happens when you're searching in your salvage haunts for one thing, you'll find some other wonderful thing. This is how many salvage artists fill in their wish list for tools.

A mosaic salvage project is more complicated, requiring lots of salvage pieces and specialized skills.

Because you're working with old objects, and perhaps experimenting with materials that you're not expert with yet, safety gear is extremely important when making salvage style projects. Always use the usual safety equipment that is specific to the particular field of salvage style, such as woodworking or welding. Wear ear protection when using power tools. And anytime you're working with objects that can splinter and fly, such as glass pieces, wear safety goggles and work slowly to avoid cutting yourself.

There is a salvage style fashion: loose-fitting work clothes with long sleeves and long pants. Necessities are sturdy work boots and protective gloves.

SALVAGE WOOD PROJECTS

For big wood projects, such as furniture and columns, you'll need basic woodworking power tools, such as a jigsaw and circular saw. Also, we assume you have

woodworking skills for these projects—they're not meant for the raw beginner. If you really don't know the difference between a butt-joint and a miter joint, then you should gain woodworking experience before you jump in. For simple salvage projects, you can get by with a handsaw and patience.

The outdoor salvage wood world is firmly divided between two camps: those who want to paint or preserve the wood in their outdoor projects and those who want to leave it natural and let it weather. Do what you want. You can always paint a project and then let it age. Or vice versa.

Paint or not, you'll probably want to fix up the wood a bit, sand its edges smooth, or burn the edges to give them more definition. If the wood is painted, you'll want to chip off the loose paint and possibly sand it to reveal more layers of paint underneath.

WORKING WITH OLD PAINT

*L*ead-based paint was widely used, both on interiors and exteriors, until the 1970s—thus architectural salvage that you consider "old" probably was painted with lead paint. You can't tell if paint has lead in it just by looking at it, and experts disagree on the effectiveness of do-it-yourself lead-testing kits. Our advice is to assume that any salvaged object painted before 1970 has lead-based paint on it.

As lead-based paint deteriorates, it can chip or crumble into dust particles. Breathing the dust particles or ingesting them can cause serious health problems, especially for children and pregnant women. That's why you need to take every measure possible to avoid creating and raising dust from lead-based paint.

With any painted salvaged object, you should always wet sand, not dry sand. Sanding with water cuts down dust particles—and also makes the job go faster.

Another solution is to paint over the lead-based paint and/or seal it with a clear polyurethane finish. Be sure to work outside or in a well-ventilated area, using water to cut down the dust. Wear a HEPA-filtered dust mask (other masks don't filter out lead). Information about lead-based paint is easy to find in libraries, home improvement stores and the Internet.

Once you have safely removed the old paint, you can easily re-paint the project with new paint. If you want to give your project a new color, and still have it look old, it's easy to create that effect. For tips on painting

wood, see the Vintage Heat Register Doormat project on page 89.

Here's how to achieve a weathered effect on tin tiles, which usually have a decorative pattern that painting emphasizes beautifully. Paint the tiles with a vibrantly colored oil-based paint, and let them dry. Then add a coat of white paint and let it set for about five minutes (humidity affects the drying time, so just keep an eye on the paint). Wipe off the raised areas to reveal the color underneath and show the detail of the tile. To get defined results, wipe the paint with a rag over your fingers. See the Stately Tin Tile Planters on page 45 as an example of this technique.

Assume old paint is lead-based and take precautions.

First of all, there are many easy ways to work with metal salvage that don't require experience or expensive tools. Sometimes all you need to do to rescue an old piece of metal is scrape off the rust with a wire brush and paint it. And sometimes not even that. See the marvelous Sturdy Metal Edging project on page 78—not a minute of scraping in the whole project!

Metal hardware, especially those pieces made of brass that gleam after polishing, are frequently used in salvage projects. It's satisfying to use old-time hardware, especially if you're a renovation purist; and it's also good to know that replicas of the old hardware are easy to find. Check out home improvement stores or renovation specialty catalogs. After you've gone salvage hunting a few times, you'll pride yourself on being able to distinguish a butterfly hinge from a Hoosier cabinet hinge or a Colonial hinge. In fact, you'll soon come to love old hardware as we do and find all kinds of uses for it in salvage style projects.

SALVAGE METAL PROJECTS

Many salvage style projects for outdoor living involve metal. The reasons are obvious: metal doesn't deteriorate outdoors as quickly as wood, and by its nature it can be shaped and bent into wonderful decorative designs. But many people shy away from metal salvage style projects because they don't know how to work with metal. What a shame. Learning about metal is one of the great adventures of making salvage style projects.

Right: Salvage metal makes sturdy edging. Center: Welding combines unlike salvage metals.

Far right: Complete cast iron pieces make stunning garden accents.

SALVAGE STYLE SAFETY

When you're working with old things, particularly with items that have sharp points, you face a serious health concern: the risk of getting tetanus, a bacterial disease that affects the nervous system. Tetanus is prevented by vaccination shots, usually given in childhood. A booster shot is required every ten years to keep the vaccination effective—something that many adults forget. Tetanus shots and boosters can be easily scheduled with your family doctor or at a local clinic.

The most effective way to prevent health or safety problems is to follow a simple safety code: "Salvage Style is Neat." Just because your work area is full of old things doesn't mean it has to be shabby. A safe and orderly work area is good for you, your visitors, and your projects.

Nineteenth-century gates are right at home in modern gardens. Keep them as gates or turn them into fantastic trellises.

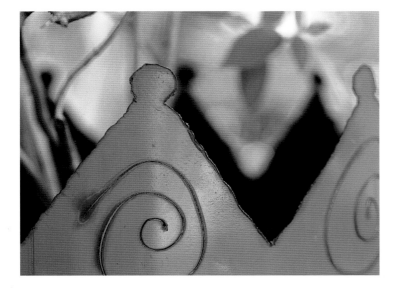

Cutting Metal

With malleable metals such as aluminum, tin, and copper, the most fun comes from cutting and bending them into shapes. If the metal sheets are really thin, you can cut them with an old pair of scissors; better yet, invest in a good pair of tin snips. If you like to cut shapes into your metal pieces, such as the metal planter edge at the left or the Fancy Flying Spindles project on page 134, you'll need another tool, a plasma cutter. Once you learn how to use the plasma cutter, you'll be grabbing every piece of metal salvage you can find to create designs in them.

To enjoy the full range of metal salvage in the garden, you do need to consider the wonderful world of welding. There are two different ways to accomplish projects that need welding.

Do it yourself. Yes, you read right. Welding might take more equipment and space than you have in your garage workshop, but it's not an impossible skill to learn. And you don't necessarily need to buy the equipment. It's easy to find welding classes that allow you to make your own projects, safely, under the supervision of an expert instructor. Welding is growing in popularity everywhere, which means it's frequently taught at art schools, trade schools, and community colleges.

Hire a welder/fabricator. Having an expert on your salvage team is a good idea. Welders are easy to find. Ask your friends for recommendations or search the phone directories. Consider choosing a welder whose shop is mobile—you can leave heavy metal salvage at your house and not have to move it back and forth to a welder's place of business. What could be easier?

WORKING WITH A WELDER/FABRICATOR: ADVICE FROM A PRO

A welder welds pieces of metal together. A welder/fabricator welds and also cuts and grinds metal pieces and can fabricate a metal project from your design.

Welding is the process of running a bead of filler metal between two other metal pieces so they all are melded, or welded, together. Welding skill is knowing the specific properties of different metals and how they respond to the process of heating and cooling. Professional welder/fabricators must know, for example, that to weld cast iron and carbon steel requires a careful decision on which metal to use as the filler metal. Cast iron is brittle and it could crack during welding, or shrink as it is being cooled, so the middle metal would have to be softer to allow for the cast iron's swelling and contracting.

Stainless steel, of course, doesn't rust; cast iron and carbon steel do. Rust does diminish the integrity of the metal, but it doesn't eliminate it from the chance to be transformed. In fact, many salvage designers prefer working with rusty metal because of its distinctive look. With rusty metal, the welder usually first grinds and cuts the metal at the welding joints so they are smooth and better prepared to take the welding.

Like other professionals, welders expect you to get several estimates, so you don't have to feel shy about doing that. Present your welder with a detailed sketch, including precise measurements. If you like the work he or she did on your project, be sure to tell your friends.

SALVAGE CONCRETE & STONE PROJECTS

Concrete and stone play big roles in outdoor landscaping. Statues, even pockmarked and with missing limbs, seem to give an aura of timelessness to the garden. Concrete slabs make wonderful benches. Sections of concrete, even the most ordinary pieces such as sections of old sidewalks, can be combined to create stunning monolithic garden sculptures. Old cut stone adds drama to every place it's used.

Plan carefully where you want to place concrete pieces. Prepare the area you want for your concrete object so the ground is level and flat. Don't try to carry heavy concrete objects yourself. Get help, or hire someone with the right equipment, including a sturdy truck and moving equipment.

To cut concrete, you need a masonry circular saw. To drill holes into concrete salvage, put a masonry bit on your power drill. Always wear protective gear when modifying pieces of concrete.

SALVAGE MOSAIC PROJECTS

If you're new to mosaic work, start small, such as by covering a birdbath bowl or tabletop with pottery shards. Then venture to more ambitious projects, adding mirror and glass pieces, such as the Mosaic Garden Panels on page 116. Supplies for outdoor mosaic work are pretty simple: a freeze/thaw stable mastic made for outdoor work into which you place the tile, trowels and sponges to spread it, and the grout that goes between the tiles.

SALVAGE CLAY PROJECTS

Clay salvage, with its weathered appearance and clinging companions of lichen and moss, is always right for the garden. You can still find larger salvage clay objects that are complete, such as a perfectly shaped chimney pot to turn into a planter or path marker, and curved terracotta roof tiles to use as edging. Broken, salvaged clay pieces can be used as decorative accents, or raised bed edging, or in your flowerpots as mulch.

If you have enough garden space to keep a lion happy—why not bring him home?

These heavily profiled nineteenth-century brick tiles would look stunning underneath a glass tabletop.

With a handheld glasscutter, you can easily re-shape pieces of broken glass and mirror.

SALVAGE GLASS AND MIRROR PROJECTS

Glass and mirrors are popular in salvage projects because of the sparkle they add to gently hued old wood. It's always nice to find whole pieces, especially glass panes, so collect them when you can and store them safely if you're not using them right away. Don't throw out broken pieces. With a simple glasscutter, you can cut them into custom-designed shapes. If the job is big, you can have the glass professionally cut. Do know that repairing old stained glass windows is becoming a lost art because of the type of leading used between the pieces, so it's worth the effort it takes to find someone who is skilled in the old ways.

If you're new to the world of architectural salvage, you might think there's something wrong with glass that is wavy. On the contrary, that's what indicates it's old and valuable. See the comments on old glass on page 126.

When inexperienced people take down an old house, they often remove only the glass part of a lighting fixture because that's the prettiest part. Now there's a glut of glass available but not enough fixture parts to hang them—remember to gather the mundane fixture parts as well.

Far right: Slate is a wonderful material that is still waiting to be discovered by salvage artists.

Glass and crystal chandelier drops, in many different shapes, are still available. Many are brand new, so it's hard to tell the difference until you look closely to see the age of the metal hangers. Colored crystals are very desirable—grab them when you find them. See the Sparkling Mobile on page 127 and the Salvage Treasures Window on page 147 for inspiration on the use of chandelier pieces.

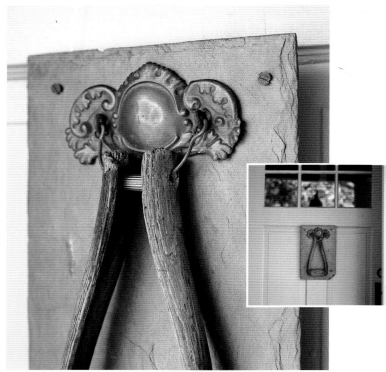

SALVAGE SLATE PROJECTS

Slate, most often found in the form of roof tiles, is actually one of the most common salvage materials available today. It's easy to work with, affordable, and weatherproof—so why aren't there more salvage artists working with it? See the marvelous Handsome Handle Door Knocker above and on page 34 for one ingenious way to use slate.

PLACING SALVAGE STYLE PROJECTS IN THE GARDEN

Remember the weather and its effects on your project. Wood will get more dried out and weathered if it's enjoying a sunbath every day. Wood projects will rot quickly if left to sit on the ground, so place them on concrete or brick. Place objects that rely on sunshine for some of their beauty, such as objects with glass, where they'll be sure to get the late afternoon light.

Projects with thin legs, such as the Garden Goddess Trellis on page 104, can topple over after a good rain has made the ground wet and mushy. It's best to keep anything with thin legs on a protective floor of concrete, brick, or wood decking.

All of your planters will last longer and be more easily moved if you don't actually fill them with dirt. Instead, put soil-filled pots inside your planter and fluff up a lot of moss to fill in the spaces.

If your salvage projects have moving metal parts, such as pinwheels or whirligigs or weather vanes, remember to keep them well lubricated throughout the seasons so they don't freeze up from rust.

DIGGING POSTHOLES

There's one aspect of making garden projects that everyone is really glad to shout "Hurray, it's over!" That's digging postholes. Here are some keys to happy posthole digging:

■ Plan and lay out your digging site carefully so you don't have to re-dig a hole.

■ Don't try to rush the process. Nothing makes it go faster.

■ Get the right equipment, such as a posthole digger. Borrow or rent it from home improvement stores if you have to.

■ Be organized. Have all the pieces of your project, all the necessary tools, protective gloves, water, and snacks at the digging site.

Always dig your postholes deep and wide enough to keep your project safely upright.

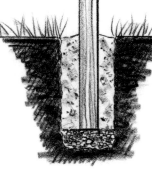

Figure 1: Posthole

Add 4 inches (10.2 cm) of gravel, then backfill with dirt. The length of the post in the ground should be one-third the height of the post above ground.

■ Don't do it by yourself. Even if you are a look-alike for Paul Bunyan, get yourself a helper. The whole process goes more efficiently when it's fun.

■ Keep the end in sight. Your project will look terrific and you'll enjoy it for many years. It will be worth all the effort to put it up.

For most salvage project postholes, we recommend the simple earth-and-gravel fill method shown in fig. 1 on page 25. This method keeps water from collecting around the posts and works fine in stable soils.

Some people prefer concrete post footings in unstable soils, and will argue that concrete grants greater post longevity. If your project is big, such as the Special Occasion Pergola on page 118, and you want to make it a permanent installation, get advice from local experts to see if concrete is recommended in your specific area.

Sizing your holes correctly is important. As a general rule, postholes should be twice as wide as the posts. For example, if a post is 18 inches (45.7 cm) wide, your hole should be 36 inches (91.4 cm) in diameter. Hole depth should be roughly one-third the height of the post above ground, plus an additional 4 inches (10.2 cm) to handle the layer of gravel below the post.

Dig each hole straight down. Once you've dug to the correct depth, shovel in the gravel into the bottom of the hole and use a spare 2 x 4 to tamp the gravel so it's level and firm.

LANDSCAPING WITH SALVAGE STYLE PROJECTS

As you can see from the photos throughout the book, salvage style projects fit beautifully in any kind of garden. The photo below left shows how wonderful classical-looking salvage objects look in gardens that run wild. In a more precisely landscaped part of the garden, below, a salvage style project adds a touch of unconventional whimsy.

About the Projects

On the following pages you'll find 41 projects with step by step instructions. The range of materials is similar to what you'll find in the world of architectural salvage: wood, metal, clay, slate, glass, and mirrors. There are 24 designers represented, ranging in experience from brand-new salvage artist to award-winning professional. In addition, we've included dozens of other salvage art pieces in our gallery sections throughout the book to inspire you.

You'll gain the most benefit from *Salvage Style for the Garden* if you read the project all the way through before starting, taking notes on what tools, materials, and skills you'll need. Many projects have specific design tips from the designers, which you can easily apply to your own projects. We also indicated in each project when we thought the weight or complexity of the project meant you'd need someone to help you.

Even though each of us has our specialty in salvage style, we encourage you to glance through all the projects and enjoy all the photos in the book. We hope you'll come to appreciate the incredible range of salvage style possibilities as much as we did. Enjoy!

MEDALLION SUNDIAL

BEFORE SALVAGE DESIGNER PHILLIP PRICE COMBINED THEM, THE PARTS OF THIS MARVELOUS SUNDIAL HAD LIVES FROM DIFFERENT TIMES. THE ROUND SUNDIAL FACE WAS A CEILING MEDALLION SALVAGED FROM A HOUSE BUILT IN 1879. THE GNOMÓN (THE UPRIGHT PART THAT CASTS A SHADOW AS THE SUN MAKES ITS PATH ACROSS THE SKY) WAS AN OLD STREET SIGN BRACKET. VINTAGE HANDCUT NAILS BECAME ROMAN NUMERALS. THE BASE, FOUND IN A LANDFILL, HAD BEEN THE SUPPORT OF A BIRDBATH. HAVE FUN USING YOUR OWN SALVAGE PIECES.

MATERIALS

Large, round, flat salvaged object, suitable for a sundial face

Salvaged piece of metal or wood scrollwork with two flat sides, high enough to act as a gnomon and cast a shadow across the sundial face

Handcut nails or other materials to shape the Roman numerals

Copper wire and/or tacks to make decorative trim

Base of a birdbath or other pedestal

Bolts or screws

All-weather adhesive glue

Satin polyurethane spray

INSTRUCTIONS

1 Drill two holes through the gnomon into the sundial face and attach with the screws. (On a sundial, you won't really get the accurate time unless you match the angle of the gnomon to the line of latitude. If you want scientifically correct time, do research, and attach your gnomon at the angle you desire.)

2 Pencil-mark the placement of the nails as Roman numerals on the sundial face and attach them with all-weather adhesive glue.

3 Shape old copper wire or tacks to create decorative trim on the sundial face. If you don't have old copper wire, you can "age" new wire by searing it with a handheld flame starter. Hold the wire with protective gloves so you don't burn yourself.

4 Spray the completed sundial face with the satin polyurethane finish to protect it from the weather. Place the birdbath base where it will rest securely and set the sundial face on top of it.

TOOLS

Power drill and appropriate drill bits

I had lots of fun researching sundials before I settled on my design. It's exciting to discover the history of things, especially when you know it will apply to something you're going to make.

—PHILLIP PRICE

NEW-LIFE BIRDFEEDER

SURELY THE MAKERS OF THIS OLD ASHTRAY DIDN'T FORESEE ITS FUTURE AS A BIRDFEEDER—IT TOOK A SALVAGE STYLE ARTIST TO ENVISION A NEW AND LIFE-AFFIRMING PURPOSE FOR IT.

MATERIALS

Vintage metal pedestal ashtray

All-purpose cleaner

Masking tape

Exterior spray paint in your choice of color

Medium-grit sandpaper

TOOLS

Wire brush

INSTRUCTIONS

1 Scrub the ashtray with the cleaner and water, and let it dry. Scrape away excessive rust with the wire brush.

2 Use masking tape to cover any areas you don't want painted, such as the iron handle and the pedestal. Spray the rest with red paint to create a warm glow. Let the paint dry thoroughly. Sand the areas you want to be highlighted.

3 Wash the ashtray again to remove any excess paint dust, and let it dry.

I didn't notice the ashtray was brass until I started sanding it!

—CHRISTI WHITELEY

MATERIALS

2 pieces of slender salvaged metal

Tree limb with nice natural "arch"

Paint and paintbrushes (optional)

Wire

TOOLS

Wire cutters

SLENDER PATH ARBOR

T O PIECES OF WROUGHT IRON RESCUED FROM THE SIDE OF THE ROAD, THE DESIGNERS ADDED A TREE-LIMB ARCH FOUND IN THE GARDEN. SIMPLE, EASY, FREE—IT'S ABSOLUTELY PERFECT SALVAGE STYLE!

INSTRUCTIONS

1 Paint your arbor sides if you wish.

2 Place the arbor in a protected area where it won't get much wind. It's not meant to be very sturdy. Insert the arbor sides into the ground at least a foot (30.5 cm).

3 Wire the tree limb arch to the top of the sides. If you wish, allow lightweight plants (not heavy ones), such as clematis, to climb up the sides of the arbor.

A happy garden loves salvage projects...they remind us how new life comes from old things...

— HEATHER SPENCER

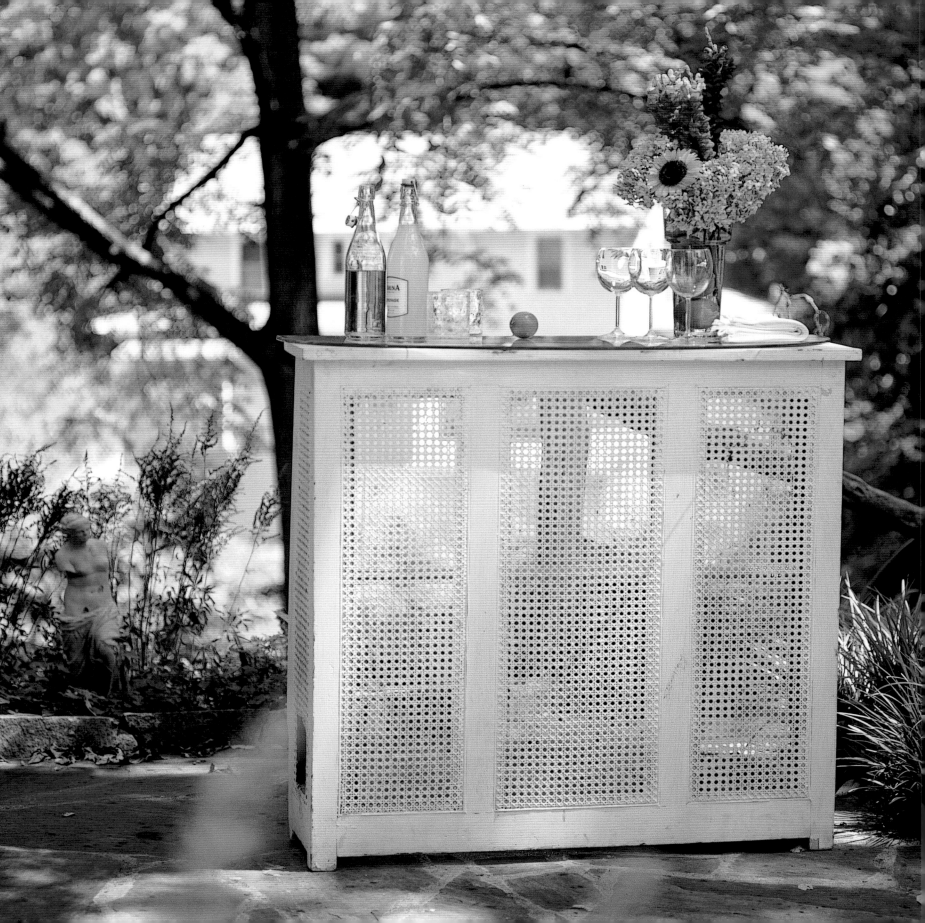

SUMMER PATIO BAR

WHILE BROWSING IN AN ARCHITECTURAL SALVAGE STORE, THE DESIGNER SPIED VINTAGE RADIATOR COVERS MADE OF WOOD AND METAL SCREEN. HE IMMEDIATELY IMAGINED SHOWING THEM OFF ON A SUMMER PATIO. A FEW AISLES AWAY, HE FOUND A STACK OF SALVAGED GLASS TABLETOPS IN ODD SIZES—VOILÀ—A COMPLETE SALVAGE SUITE IN LESS THAN TEN MINUTES!

MATERIALS

Salvaged radiator covers, any size

Salvaged glass tabletops, the thicker the glass the better

Protective felt tabs (optional)

INSTRUCTIONS

1 Once you find a suitable radiator cover, imagine it as something else. The covers come in a variety of sizes, so if you can't find one sized for an outdoor bar, consider other transformations such as display tables, patio storage cabinets, or poolside towel closets.

2 The designer loved the distressed look of the radiator cover as it was, so he didn't remove any of the rust spots or try to fix any damaged areas. But if you like things to look spiffy, then make any repairs you wish. If the register is not already white or light colored, consider painting it so it has a summery look.

3 If your radiator cover is open in the back, all you'd have to do is attach some sturdy supports and make shelves out of salvaged wood or glass.

4 The glass top protects the vintage wood from further damage and also adds an eye-catching sparkle to the whole piece. If you can't find thick glass at a reasonable price, then consider stacking two or three less expensive pieces of thin glass. Attach sticky protective felt tabs on the glass pieces to keep them from accidentally slipping off one another.

I prefer things that don't need a lot of transformation—I trust my creativity to make something from them.

— PERRI

HANDSOME HANDLE DOORKNOCKER

Amazing, isn't it, how inviting a door becomes when it's partnered with a handsome doorknocker? Here's one made of an unlikely trio—a handworn old shovel handle, a vintage drawer pull, and a slate roof tile.

INSTRUCTIONS

1 Lay the handle and the escutcheon on the slate, marking the location of the eyes with the pencil. Drill two holes in the slate at the marks. (The two holes near the top edges of the slate are already there, used previously to attach the tile to the roof.)

2 Thread the two eyes through the escutcheon and the holes you drilled for them in slate tile. Secure them on the back with nuts that fit them. (If necessary, cut off any excess length of the eyes so the knocker will hang flush to the door.)

3 Attach the small hinge to the back of the shovel handle with screws so that it doesn't show, but will "click" when it's struck on the slate.

4 Place the spacer between the holes in the shovel handle and thread wire from one hole through the spacer to the other hole, using the pliers to make a loop on either end to attach the wire to the eyes. (See the photo for guidance.) If you're using the wire from the drawer pull handle, first use the needle-nose pliers to straighten the wire enough to thread it.

5 Attach the knocker to the door with screws through the hanging holes. Use old screws if you have them because they'll look more appropriate than new screws.

We had this broken shovel handle that was so old and neat looking, we just couldn't throw it out. We wanted it to knock against something that would make noise but not rot from being outside. That's when we thought of slate—a perfect match.

—CHRISTI WHITELEY

MATERIALS

Shovel handle

Drawer pull with an escutcheon, with
two eyes and a wire handle (if you
can find only the escutcheon back,
just purchase two separate eyes, and
make a handle using baling wire)

Slate roof tile

Small hinge and screws

Spacer made of anything with a hole
in the middle, such as an old piece of
gold-colored, ribbed plastic tubing

2 nuts to fit on the eyes of the
escutcheon

TOOLS

Pencil

Power drill with masonry bit

Needle-nose pliers

Screwdriver

DESIGN TIP

THE KNOCKER IS ATTRACTIVE BECAUSE IT USES A
VARIETY OF MATERIALS AND SHAPES IN A PLEASING
WAY. FOR ALL OBJECTS, BUT PARTICULARLY THOSE
THAT WILL BE LOOKED AT OFTEN AND NEAR EYE
LEVEL, CHOOSE YOUR PIECES CAREFULLY.

COOL-WHITE PEDESTAL TABLES

A FTER YOU REMOVE THE BOWL FROM A VINTAGE CAST IRON BATHROOM SINK, WHAT REMAINS IS THE HOLLOW PEDESTAL WITH ITS GRACEFUL UPSWEEP. ADD GLASS TOPS TO CREATE SENSATIONAL COOL-WHITE TABLES.

INSTRUCTIONS

1 Select a sink pedestal with a wide top and a flat bottom that will rest safely on the ground.

2 With the wrench and other tools as needed, remove the sink and its parts. Recycle them or set them aside for other salvage projects.

3 Work in an area with good ventilation. With a strong but non-abrasive cleaner, remove grease and any other debris. If there are noticeable nicks, cover them with white enamel touch-up paint.

4 To make the backside of the pedestal attractive, disguise it with potted plants or high-growing grasses.

5 If you want to create displays under glass tabletops, first fill the gap in the back of the pedestal with a metal sheet so you have a solid cavity. Then build up the space in the cavity, such as with potting soil or with rocks or empty flower pots placed upside down one on top of the other. Place your display where it will rest just under the top of the glass.

6 Glue protective felt tabs to the metal edge of the pedestals and place the glass on top of them.

MATERIALS

Cast iron sink with nicely shaped pedestal

Glass tabletop to suit the pedestal shape and size

Metal sheet to fill the empty back of the pedestal

Pretty objects to create a decorative display under the glass

Non-abrasive cleaner

White enamel touch-up paint

Glue

Protective felt tabs

TOOLS

Wrench and other tools as needed to remove the sink from the pedestal

Small paintbrush

A hollow pedestal under glass invites all kinds of creative opportunities... fill it with flowers, or beautiful rocks, or brightly colored autumn leaves, or holiday ornaments, or mini-lights at night...

— DANA M. IRWIN

To make a birdbath, fit a large, shallow dish on top of the pedestal.

DESIGN BY DANA M. IRWIN

Thick glass makes a sturdy tabletop and allows a beautiful display to be seen underneath it.

DESIGN BY DANA M. IRWIN

Old concrete and new hardware make a sensational sundial.

COURTESY OF UNIQUITIES ARCHITECTURAL ANTIQUES

A nineteenth-century pigs' trough becomes a tabletop birdfeeder.

A Victorian terra-cotta roof finial becomes a regal garden accent.

Instead of having a window on the garden, put a window in the garden.

Vintage tin tiles are so pretty, you can use them by themselves to brighten up any spot in your garden.

DESIGN BY BRADLEY BARRETT

May all our holiday gifts be as beautiful and simple as this one!

DESIGN BY SIMONE WILSON

CUTTING EDGE COPPER KETTLE PLANTERS

GIANT COPPER KETTLES WERE RESCUED FROM A GRAND OLD HOTEL UNDERGOING RENOVATION. THEY HAD BEEN FLATTENED AS REFUSE BEFORE DESIGNER BRADLEY BARRETT PRIED THEM APART TO MAKE THEM ROUND AGAIN. TOPPING THE KETTLE RIMS ARE VINTAGE TWO-MAN SAWS, ONCE USED TO FELL TREES IN THE NEARBY MOUNTAINS.

MATERIALS

1 old saw blade from a two-man saw

1 big copper kettle (the ones in the photo are 20 inches [50.8 cm] tall and 24 inches [61 cm] in diameter) or other metal container

8 decorative metal finials, such as those for lamps

Bolts and washers, as needed, to match the size of the holes in the saw blade

8 bolts and washers, to match the size of the finials

River pebbles or gravel to fill the kettle

Potted plant to place into the kettle

Moss (optional)

TOOLS

Protective safety gloves

Power drill with drill bits to match the sizes of the bolts

Helper needed to assist holding the blade in step 2

The finials are decorative on the outside of the kettle and functional inside.

After the two ends of the sawblade have been bolted together, the curved blade rests on the end of the finial inside the kettle.

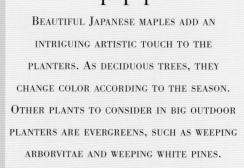

INSTRUCTIONS

1 Make one planter at a time, starting with the saw blade. Select the sizes of your bolts, washers, and drill bits to match the width of the holes on both ends of the saw blade where it was once attached to its wooden handles.

2 Bend the saw blade into a circle. If you have experience handling saw blades, you can make this project by yourself. Otherwise, because the saw blade could snap back unexpectedly, have your helper hold the blade ends together while you secure them. Be sure you and your helper wear thick protective gloves. Using the bolts and washers, securely attach the two ends together. Set the curved blade aside for now while you work on the kettle.

3 Drill eight holes evenly spaced around the top of the copper kettle 2 inches (5 cm) below the rim. Add bolts and washers as needed and insert the finials into the holes. If the curved sawblade is shorter than the circumference of the kettle, you'll need to use longer bolts (and more washers) to extend the support farther into the center of the kettle.

4 Add a layer of stone or gravel to the bottom of the kettle. Place the potted plant and surround it with more stones. Gently rest the sawblade on top of the finial's nuts-and-bolts supports inside the rim of the kettle.

MARILYN DRABICKI & LARRY FREER

RUSTY STAR PLANTER

E VEN IF YOU CAN'T WELD, YOU CAN MAKE WONDERFUL METAL PROJECTS IF YOU HAVE A FRIEND WHO DOES. DIVIDE THE CREATIVE PROCESS AS MARILYN AND LARRY DO: SHE FINDS THE OBJECTS AND USES HER ARTISTIC EYE TO RE-IMAGINE THEM, AND HE DOES THE ACTUAL WELDING. EASY!

MATERIALS

Fitting from the top of an old fuel oil drum or something similar, with a hinged cap

Cast iron "star" that was used to secure a building's metal reinforcing rods

Gravel

Potting soil

Slow-growing plants

TOOLS

Welding equipment

INSTRUCTIONS

W eld the cap open so it will hold the candle. Weld the bottom of the fitting to the center of the star. Place a layer of gravel, then add soil and plants to the fitting. That's it!

I never really dealt with anything creative before I started making salvage projects with Marilyn. Her artistic perspective got me going. Now I look at a piece of iron and draw up my own ideas.

– LARRY FREER

STATELY TIN TILE PLANTERS

THE BEAUTIFUL TIN TILES THAT DESIGNER SIMON WHITELEY RESCUED WERE ONCE THE CEILING OF A RESTAURANT BUILT IN THE 1920S. FORMED IN TWO-PANEL SHEETS, THE TILE WAS LARGER THAN MOST SALVAGED TILES AND PERFECT FOR BENDING— GIVING SIMON THE IDEA TO BEND THEM AROUND A BOX TO MAKE BIG PLANTERS. YOU CAN DO THE SAME WITH TILES OF ANY SIZE.

MATERIALS

2 two-panel sections of tin tile, 2 feet (.6 m) square

Scrap wood, pre-cut in pieces to make a square box

All-purpose cleaner

Nails appropriate for the scrap wood

Wood sealer

Protective gloves (tin tile can be sharp!)

1-inch (2.54 cm) nails, as needed

Exterior paint

TOOLS

Nailer or hammer

Mallet (optional)

Paintbrush

Paint rag (optional)

INSTRUCTIONS

1 Wash the tin tile and scrap wood with the cleaner and let everything dry.

2 Nail the scrap wood together to form a 2-foot (.6 m) square box with four sides and a bottom. Keep it open at the top. Coat the wood with the wood sealer.

3 Wearing the protective gloves, wrap one of the two-panel sections of tin tile around two sides of the box. Nail it onto the first edge, then bend the tile by creasing it around the next corner. Secure it with nails at its end, which would be the third corner of the box.

4 Nail the next tile starting at the third corner, just covering the end of the first tile. Repeat step 3, bend-ing the tile and nailing it in place at the corner where you started the first piece of tin.

5 Using the hammer or mallet, bang all the sharp tin edges flat and wrap the top edge of the tile over the planter's rim at the open end, and then tack it down with the 1-inch (2.54 cm) nails.

6 If you plan to leave the boxes out-side, place them on concrete and line them with heavy plastic stapled to the interior. Keep them off the ground and they can last for years.

Most people buy small tin tiles because they can be cut up into decorative items. I prefer to make projects with big tiles and keep them intact to show off the full beauty of the tin.

SIMON WHITELEY

GORGEOUS GLASS HANGING PLANTERS

T HE UNDERSIDE OF HANGING PLANTERS IS ORDINARILY ONE OF A GARDEN'S LEAST ATTRACTIVE SIGHTS. NOT ANYMORE—IT'S "BOTTOMS UP!" WHEN YOU TRANSFORM VINTAGE GLASS LIGHT FIXTURES INTO GORGEOUS HANGING FLOWER BASKETS.

BEFORE YOU START

You'll probably have to order the "ball end" lengths of chain new from a lighting store since they are only rarely found with an old fixture. Make sure the threaded loop fastener fits the rosette without slipping through, so take the rosette with you when you are looking for the fastener. In the stores, ball chain comes on a roll, which sales associates can cut to length for you. Or you can buy long pieces of chain and cut it yourself with tin snips or wire cutters.

INSTRUCTIONS

1 In essence, you'll be re-hanging the fixtures similarly to the way it was originally hung, but with a much longer chain so the glass can be filled with flowers and enjoyed. Thread the three short "ball end" sections of chain through the holes on the glass from the outside. (These ball ends only come in short lengths, so you don't need to have them cut.)

2 With the connectors, link the three short "ball end" sections to the three long lengths of chain now on the inside of the fixture.

3 Thread the connected chains through each hole of doorknob rosette. Add the "bell ends "on the other side of the rosette (these don't show). These will keep the chains from slipping out and will hold everything together.

4 Put the threaded loop fastener through the large hole in the rosette, so the loop is on the top. Secure it with the washer on the underside.

5 Fill the fixture with floral moss and flowers and hang it from the loop where the beauty of the glass can be seen easily.

MATERIALS

Vintage glass light fixture cover with three evenly spaced holes

3 short "ball end" lengths of ball chain (may need to order new)

3 connectors for ball chain

3 identical lengths of ball chain cut to the length you want the planter to hang

3 "bell ends" for ball chains (shaped like a bell or tulip)

1 old doorknob rosette (similar to an escutcheon) with 3 holes

1 threaded loop fastener (it has a loop on one side and is threaded on the other with a threaded washer)

Floral moss

Flowers

TOOLS

Tin snips or wire cutters (optional)

SHUTTER-SLAT VENEER PLANTERS

WHAT A CLEVER WAY TO RECYCLE PERFECTLY GOOD WOOD THAT MOST FOLKS JUST THROW AWAY—USE LOOSE SHUTTER SLATS TO CONSTRUCT BEAUTIFULLY PATTERNED VENEERS. THEN COVER ORDINARY WOODEN BOXES WITH THE VENEERS TO MAKE SPECTACULAR PLANTERS.

MATERIALS

Shutter slats, enough to cover the box (you can find them everywhere once you start looking)

Wooden box, such as a crate or old drawer

Scrap trim wood

All-purpose cleaner

Paint or stain to match the color of the slats

TOOLS

Saw

Nail gun and nails, or staple gun and staples

INSTRUCTIONS

1 Scrub the slats with the cleaner and water, and let them dry

2 Lay out the slats on one side of the box. Design a pattern if you like with vertical and horizontal slats. But don't cut the slats lengthwise, since that would ruin the attractive consistent width of the slats.

3 Cut the slats to the desired lengths and angles. If the shutter was actually functional, each slat will have nibs or tips at the end. If you're using the whole length of the slat, just cut the nibs off. (If the shutter was just decorative there won't be nibs.)

4 Use the nail gun or the staple gun to attach the slats securely onto the wood on all the sides of the box.

5 Give a finished look to the opening of the box by cutting scrap trim wood at 45° angles to the lengths needed for each side of the opening. Staple the trim in place. Paint or stain it to match the slats.

6 Put the plant in its own container and then place it in the box. This will help the wood last a lot longer outdoors.

DESIGN TIP

IN ADDITION TO BEING PLANTERS, VENEER-COVERED BOXES HAVE ALL KINDS OF USES IN THE GARDEN. TURN THEM UPRIGHT AS STORAGE BOXES FOR TALL ITEMS SUCH AS GARDEN TOOLS. PUT LIDS ON THEM TO MAKE OUTDOOR CHESTS FOR SANDBOX AND POOL TOYS. TOP THEM WITH GLASS TO BECOME WONDERFUL PATIO TABLES.

GOOD MORNING FLOWER BED

WHAT A GLORIOUS WAY FOR FLOWERS TO WAKE UP AND GREET THE MORNING SUN—IN A REAL FLOWER BED! THE BED IS EASILY FASHIONED OUT OF SALVAGED BEDSPRINGS AND WOOD POSTS. AS DESIGNER ANNE KAUFMAN DID, MAKE A LIVING QUILT OF POTTED MARIGOLDS AND ADD A MOSSY PILLOW.

"You can use anything salvaged to make a pretty planter or a one-of-a kind landscape sculpture. Be open to all the possibilities that come from salvaged objects."

— ANNE KAUFMANN

MATERIALS

3 wooden tomato stakes

2 fenceposts for the head posts, pre-cut to about 5 feet (1.5 m) tall

2 fenceposts for the foot posts, pre-cut to about 3 feet (.9 m) tall

1 salvaged bedspring (double- bed bed-size is ideal)

1 piece of salvaged 1 x 4 (actual size:19 mm x 89 mm) for the footboard

3-inch (7.6 cm) wood screws, as needed

14-gauge wire, as needed

Barbed wire and/or salvaged odds and ends to decorate

Small terra-cotta pots, as many as you want to put in the bedspring

Other pots as needed for the headboard

Flowers and potting soil for the pots

Moss (such as Spanish moss) to make the pillow

TOOLS

Handsaw

Power drill

Wire cutters

Helper as needed to help lift and carry

INSTRUCTIONS

1 With the saw, cut one of the tomato stakes into four small pieces to use on the inside of each of the four bedposts to support the bedsprings. Screw them each piece into place. (Use stronger supports if you plan to make the bedspring heavier by using-with more decorations or bigger pots.)

2 Use the remaining two tomato stakes to create a decorative headboard, attaching them to the insides of the headposts with the wood screws.

3 Using the wood screws, attach the 1 x 4 as a footboard to the insides of the two footposts.

4 With your helper, gently set the bedsprings on the tomato stake supports. Attach the bedsprings to the posts using the wire and screws as needed.

5 Fill the terra- cotta pots with potting soil and plants and insert them into the bedspring coils. To attract butterflies to your flowerbed, plant such annuals as sweet alyssum, salvia, or nicotiana. To attract more butterflies, put plants they love nearby, such as butterfly bushes, lilac, lavender and viburnum.

6 Make the pillow by shaping a large pile of dried moss. Embed pots of flowers in it. Add any decorative touches you wish with barbed wire and other salvaged pieces.

7 Water the small pots as needed, daily if the weather is hot and sunny.

Old fireplace grates are easy to find and make perfect planters.

DESIGN BY BRADLEY BARRETT

Pack the grates with moss, then add flowers. Or fill them with potted flowers.

DESIGN BY CHRISTI WHITELEY

Two unlikely partners make a great duo—salvage metal planters and a beautiful weathered lady.

PHOTO BY HANS ZEEGERS, SANOMA SYNDICATION

A simple salvage wood box, cut to any height you wish, will make a planter that grows more beautiful with age.

DESIGN BY BRADLEY BARRETT

Victorian chimney pot planters give an elegant touch to any garden.

DESIGN BY PEEPLES-KIMAK DESIGN ASSOCIATES

Design
BRADLEY BARRETT

ANDIRON CHILDREN'S BENCH

ANDIRONS HOLD HEAVY LOGS ON THE HORIZONTAL BARS MOUNTED BETWEEN THEIR SHORT LEGS IN THE BACK AND VERTICAL RODS IN THE FRONT. THEY MAKE GREAT LEGS FOR A STURDY CHILDREN'S BENCH.

MATERIALS

Large chunk of lumber (the thicker the wood, the more stable the bench)

Pair of vintage andirons

Wood stain or preservative (optional)

Wood screws, about $1^1/_2$ to 2 inches (3.8 to 5 cm) long, as needed

TOOLS

Saw

Router

Power drill and drill bit

Torch or heatgun (optional)

INSTRUCTIONS

1 Cut your wood to size to fit it securely and attractively on the andiron supports.

2 Use the router to make beveled or radius edges at the top. Stain the wood or use a wood preservative to give it a protective coat.

3 Cover up any fresh cuts on the wood with a natural looking "burn," using a metal cutting torch turned to low heat. If you don't have a torch and you're patient, use a heat-gun.

4 In the horizontal back support part of the andirons, drill two holes with diameters slightly larger than the screws

5 Turn the wood to its underside and set the andirons upside-down on top of it. Drive the wood screws through the holes in the andirons and into the wood.

Look at a cast-off and say: what could it be?

– BRADLEY BARRETT

PANEL-DOOR GARDEN BENCH

P ANELED WOOD DOORS HAVE STILES, OR SIDES, THAT FRAME THE PANELS. THESE STILES GIVE A DOOR SUPERB STRENGTH WHEN YOU TURN IT ON ITS SIDE TO BECOME A BENCH. AS SALVAGE MASTER SIMON WHITELEY DID, CUT A PRETTY OLD DOOR INTO TWO PIECES TO MAKE THE BENCH SEAT AND THE BACKREST, AND ADD PORCH BALUSTER LEGS AND RAFTER-TAIL ARMRESTS. THEN SHOW OFF YOUR SALVAGE STYLE WITH A FLOURISH OF DECORATIVE TRIM.

*We had a lot of doors and we wanted to do something with them besides just make tables.
A bench? But how to make it so it didn't look clunky? So we came up with the idea of using
the balusters to create an open feel to the bottom——it worked!*

–SIMON WHITELEY

MATERIALS

1 old six-panel door, 32 to 36 inches
(812.8 to 914.4 mm) wide

Balusters, as many as needed, to make 3 baluster-sets as
legs (In the bench in the photo, we used 6 balusters in
each leg, for a total of 18 balusters.)

11 lengths of 1-inch (25.4 mm) scrap wood,
cut as follows:

> 9 should match the width of the bench seat (3
> as parts of the bench seat frame, and 6 as top
> and bottom frames of the 3 baluster-sets)

> 2 should match the length of the bench seat as
> the length of its frame

Trim molding, enough to go around the perimeter of
the bench seat

3 rafter tails, or other pieces of wood, for arm rests,

2 pieces of decorative gingerbread, or scraps cut
to your own design

3 L-brackets for the armrests

2 flat metal braces to stabilize the decorative trim

Wood screws and nails as needed

All-purpose cleaner used with water

Brush

All-weather wood glue

White paint for touch-up

TOOLS

Trim saw

Sander or sandpaper

Tape measure

Chalk line

Table saw

Power drill with bits as needed

Finish nail gun

INSTRUCTIONS

1 Wash all the parts with the cleaner
and water, brushing off any loose
debris. Let everything dry.

2 Many old doors have been cut
on an angle to accommodate a
sloping floor. Square the door up
with the trim saw to the width of the
top stile of the door.

3 The bottom stile of door is usually wider than the top stile. But
when you turn the door on its side,
you want the top and bottom stiles to
be equal widths. So measure and cut
the bottom stile to match the top one.

4 You'll cut the door into two
pieces to become the seat and
the backrest. Measure and mark the
door to a width of 16 to 18 inches
(406.4 to 457.2 mm) for the seat.
Make a chalk line down the length of
the door to guide your cut. On the
table saw, cut the door lengthwise at a
45°angle.

5 Take the seat section you just cut
off and flip it over lengthwise on
your flat working surface. Apply glue
all the way down the length of the

seat on the cut edge. With your helper, raise the backrest to meet the seat and hold it in place while you nail the two pieces together. Mark the location of the three armrests (placed on the stiles, not on the panels) that you'll attach in step 11 and screw in the three L-brackets at the marks. Doing this now will also help stabilize the backrest.

6 Make the frame for the bench seat out of the 1-inch (254 mm) scrap wood, then attach it underneath the perimeter of the seat. There will be three crosspieces and 2 sidepieces.

7 Seats are usually between 17 and 19 inches (431.8 to 482.6 mm) above the ground. Here's how to arrive at the height your balusters should be cut to suit your desired height for the bench seat. Factor four other measurements: the thickness of the door (meaning its height when it's laid on its side), the thickness of the frame underneath the door, and the heights of the wood used for the top and bottom frames of the baluster-sets that you'll make in the next step. Take these four measurements and subtract the total from the height above ground that you want the seat of the bench to be. Cut even amounts from both ends of the balusters to that length.

8 Make the three baluster sets by using the finish nailer to nail the appropriate number of balusters to the top and bottom pre-cut pieces of 1-inch (254 mm) scrap. How many balusters you need depends on how wide they are and how wide the door is. The project in the photo used six balusters for each set.

9 Center one of the baluster-sets as the middle leg under the center stile (not on a panel!). Then place the other two baluster-sets under the end stiles on opposite sides of the door (again, not on a panel). Using the finish nailer and going through the top of the frame, nail the tops of the baluster sets to it.

10 Cut trim molding at 45º angles at the corners to go under the seat perimeter and cover the top of the baluster legs. Use the finish nailer to attach the trim. (This will also hide the frame.)

11 Make the armrests. You can use any scrap wood you have and cut a decorative design into it. The one in the picture was made with three old rafter tails. Use the finish nailer to secure the armrests to the seat back and seat backrests over the L-brackets that you placed in step 5.

12 Using any scrap wood you wish, make the decorative trim on the top of the backrest. The fleurs-de-lis in the photo were scraps of Victorian gingerbread trim. Attach the pieces with the finish nailer. Then add stability to the decoration by screwing one of the flat metal braces onto the back of each one, attaching the other end to the seat back.

13 Use white paint to disguise the new cuts in the old wood. Be sure to wipe it away before it dries so it looks as if it has always been there.

14 With the sander or sandpaper, smooth the edge of the seat to make it rounded and comfortable. Also sand any other places that are rough.

SMALL GARDEN SHELVES

Small outdoor shelves make good use of short pieces of salvaged wood. Leave the shelves open to show the garden behind them, or cover their backs with salvaged pressed tin. Either way the shelves are charming, useful, and oh-so-easy to make.

INSTRUCTIONS

1 Based on the width of the individual boards, decide the most suitable height and width of your shelves. The shelves in the photo are $4^1/2$ inches (11.4 cm) wide, so a good proportion for the finished project was 26 inches (60 cm) tall and 10 inches (25.4 cm) wide.

2 There are five pieces: the top, the two sides, and the two shelves. Measure and mark each piece. With the saw, cut each piece to length, and sand the ends that will be exposed. (If you want more color on the wood, paint and sand the boards now.)

3 Measure and mark where you'll place the wood screws on the top and sides of the bookcase. Screw in from the sides. Use your right-angle guide or speed square to make sure all boards are perpendicular and square.

MATERIALS

Tongue-and-groove flooring or wallboards, preferably still covered with paint in lively colors

Sandpaper

Paint (optional)

Wood screws, about $1^1/2$ to 2 inches (3.8 to 5 cm) long, as needed

TOOLS

Handsaw

Paintbrush (optional)

Drill with Phillips head bit

Right-angle guide or speed square

It's easy to add a pressed-tin back. Measure, cut the tin with tin snips, drill holes, and attach the tin with flathead nails to the top and sides of the shelf. If you wish, decorate the sides with shapes cut from scraps of tin.

BARN WOOD
ADIRONDACK CHAIRS

ANYONE CAN MAKE LOVELY PROJECTS FROM SALVAGED WOOD. BEING IMPERFECT ITSELF, THE WOOD IS WONDERFULLY FORGIVING OF A BEGINNER'S MISTAKES. THE GREY PATINA OF THE WOOD USED TO BUILD THESE CLASSIC ADIRONDACK CHAIRS CAME FROM BEING ON THE SIDE OF A BARN FOR ALMOST A CENTURY.

My favorite material to work with is antique lumber, especially barn wood. I love the silvery grey color it has. Barn wood takes no preparation to turn it into outdoor wood furniture, so I take full advantage of how easy it is to make things with it.

— BRADLEY BARRETT

MATERIALS

Nails and wood screws or bolts needed. (Regular nails will eventually rust and look compatible with unpreserved wood. Galvanized nails won't rust.)

Wood stain (optional)

Wood preservative (optional)

TOOLS

Circular saw

Sander (or sandpaper)

Hammer

Clamps

Measuring tape and marker

CUTTING LIST

Code	Item	Qty.	Dimensions
A	Arm	2	28" (711.2 mm) long, Template A. Flip pattern over for opposite arm
B	Arm Support	2	20" (508 mm) long
C	Back Legs	2	40" (1016 mm) long, Template C
D	Upper Back Brace	2	20" (508 mm) long
E	Seat Slats	8	20" x 2^1/$_2$" (508 x 63.5 mm)
F	Lower Back Support	1	22" x 2^1/$_2$" (558.8 x 63.5 mm) as thick as possible, Template F
G	Upper Back Support	1	20" x 2^1/$_2$" (508 x 63.5 mm), Template G
H	Chair Back		Cut as many pieces as needed to create a back at least 30" (762 mm) high and 20" (508 mm) wide
I	Arm Brace	2	6" x 3"(152 x 76.2 mm), if needed, Template I

INSTRUCTIONS

1 Pre-cut your pieces according to the cutting list. Sand the wood smooth where needed. Use the hammer and nails to assemble all the pieces, using clamps to hold them together as necessary while you work. Add carriage bolts as necessary for extra security where indicated.

2 Using the hammer and nails, and clamps as needed, assemble the first section: the arms (A), arm supports (B), back legs (C), and the upper back braces (D). If you are using thick pieces of wood, use carriage bolts to attach the arm supports (B) and the back legs (C), and arms (A) to the upper chair back braces (D).

3 Measure and mark on the back legs (C) the placement for the seat slats (E), leaving about a ^{1}/$_2$-inch (12.7 mm) gap between the slats to comfortably follow the curve of the back leg (C). See the photo for guidance. Put the slats aside for now.

4 Measure the thickness of the pieces of wood that will be in the chair back (H). The pieces should all be the same thickness, even though their widths and heights can vary. This thickness will be the distance between the last seat slat (E) and the lower back support (F). Nail the lower support (F) and the upper back support (G) into the two back legs (C).

5 Assemble the pieces of the chair back (H), being careful that the

combined width of the pieces will fit exactly into the space between the two arms (A), in this case, 20" (508 mm). Nail the bottoms of the chair back pieces (H) into the lower back support (F). Also nail the pieces into the upper back braces (D).

6 Nail the chair slats (E) to the back legs (C) at the marks you made in step 3.

7 If your wood is thin, add the arm braces cut from template I.

8 When finished constructing the chairs, you can stain them and apply preservative if you wish. Or just leave them in their natural state to continue to age gracefully.

Templates for Barn Wood Andirondack Chair

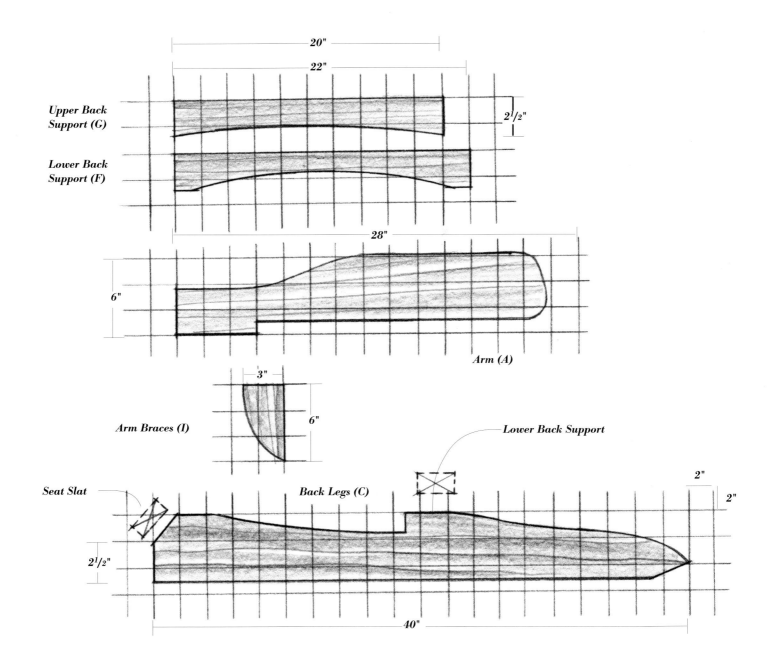

20"

22"

Upper Back
Support (G)

2¹/₂"

Lower Back
Support (F)

28"

6"

Arm (A)

3"

6"

Arm Braces (I)

Lower Back Support

Seat Slat

Back Legs (C)

2"

2"

2¹/₂"

40"

Note: See cutting list on page 64 for metric dimensions.

Barn Wood Andirondack Chair

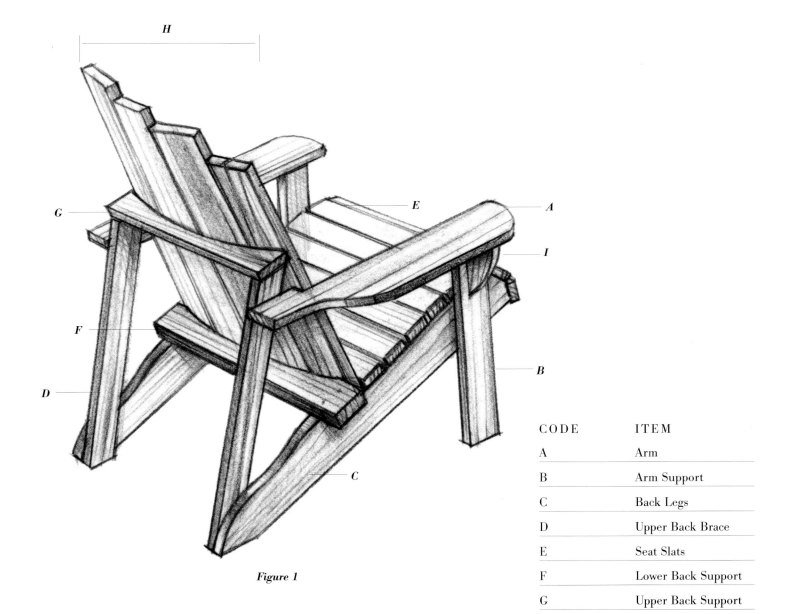

Figure 1

CODE	ITEM
A	Arm
B	Arm Support
C	Back Legs
D	Upper Back Brace
E	Seat Slats
F	Lower Back Support
G	Upper Back Support
H	Chair Back
I	Arm Brace

KING-SIZE SCRAP YARD STEEL BENCH

SCRAP YARD STEEL IS ONE OF DESIGNER BRADLEY BARRETT'S MANY SOURCES OF INSPIRATION. HERE'S ONE OF HIS FAVORITE PIECES—A HIGH, GOLD-PAINTED BENCH WITH A MARBLE SEAT SALVAGED FROM A DEPARTMENT STORE BATHROOM.

MATERIALS

Scrap yard steel, enough for the bench-back-with-legs piece, the two front legs, and the decorative wrap-around seat support

Slab of marble, stone, or wood of benchseat size

TOOLS

Oxy/acetylene torch

Grinder

Electric arc welder or a welder

INSTRUCTIONS

1 Using the following dimensions as a guide, measure and mark all your pieces:

■ The marble slab seat determined the bench's other measurements.

The slab was 48 inches (1.22 m) in length, suitable for two people sitting side-by-side. It was narrow, only 12 inches (30.5 cm) wide.

■ The benchback-with-legs piece was a pallet rack. At 45 inches (1.06 m) in height, it made a good, solid backrest. It was 42 inches (1.1 m) long, which meant the marble seat stuck out a bit at the sides. That's okay.

■ Normal seat height is about 18 inches (45.7 cm) from the ground. Brad made it a higher, more throne-like height of 25 inches (63.5 cm). This included the two front legs at 24 inches (61 cm) high and the 1-inch (2.5 cm) thickness of the marble seat.

■ The decorative punched steel piece is 63 inches (1.6 m), long enough to wrap around the front and sides of the bench and support the marble.

2 Using the torch, cut the two front legs to length and bend the punched steel piece into the wrap-around seat support.

3 Use the grinder to prepare the metal at the points you want to weld.

4 Weld the punched steel seat support to the benchback piece, then to the front legs.

5 Paint the metal surfaces with gold spray paint and let it dry thoroughly. Add a bit of royal red to the decorative piece. Rest the marble slab on the seat support. Sit back and feel noble.

Scrap metal is never perfect or straight. If things are a little crooked on the metal parts—as long as the bench seat is straight, and the structure is safe and sturdy—it's okay.

— BRADLEY BARRETT

WINDOW-LEG TABLE

A WEATHERED DOOR TOP AND LEGS MADE OF WINDOWS ARRANGED IN A ZIG ZAG PATTERN—THEY'RE SUCH SIMPLE ELEMENTS IN AN EASY, ELEGANT TABLE.

MATERIALS

3 old windows all the same height (and no more than 3 inches [7.6 cm] wider than the width of the door)

Old wooden door

Cleaning supplies

Sandpaper

Acrylic paint in various colors

Fresh leaves in a variety of shapes

Trim screws, 2¼ inches (5.7 cm) long

Weatherproof glue

TOOLS

Stiff bristle brush

Paintbrushes

Power drill screwdriver with square drive bit

Helper needed to lift door and arrange window frames

INSTRUCTIONS

1 Clean the windows thoroughly, removing any loose paint with water and the bristle brush. Sand as needed.

2 Decorate the windows in any way you wish, remembering that the door tabletop will shade the view of the windows, so you might favor light colors. Here's how to re-create the dramatic multi-dimension effect Kitty and Michael achieved: Brush fresh leaves with paint and press them onto the glass. Allow the paint to dry. Carefully remove the leaves, leaving their impression on the glass. On the opposite side of the window, brush a lighter color all over the glass so it looks like mist. Let it dry, then make and apply more leaf images until you achieve the design you want.

3 Set up the windows at 90° angles to each other in a zigzag pattern. Attach them together with the screws.

4 Set the old door on top of the windows. Wiggle the windows to fit so that they are completely under the door. Have your helper assist you to carefully lift the door off the windows so as not to disturb their arrangement. Apply glue to the top of the windows and place the door back on them. Screw the door into the window frames.

New things just can't duplicate the vintage, lived-with look of salvage objects. Each piece has a story to tell and you wonder what it is.

— KITTY BROWN

Salvage Style
GARDEN FURNITURE GALLERY

Welding transforms salvaged metal from old railings and grates into sophisticated and stylish garden tables.
DESIGNS BY PEEPLES-KIMAK DESIGN ASSOCIATES

These sturdy high chairs, a variation of the traditional Adirondack chairs, are perfect for poolside.

Pieces of weathered barn wood are the tabletop. The legs and frame are welded from salvaged steel rebar.

A solid plank of wood, heavy enough to need two people to carry, makes this evocative tabletop. The legs and frame, welded from salvaged steel rebar, were designed specifically to support the plank.

A thick piece of old lumber and salvaged metal legs make this lovely display bench.

ALL DESIGNS BY BRADLEY BARRETT

PRETTY & PRACTICAL
Projects

CLEVER LATTICE-WOOD BOXES

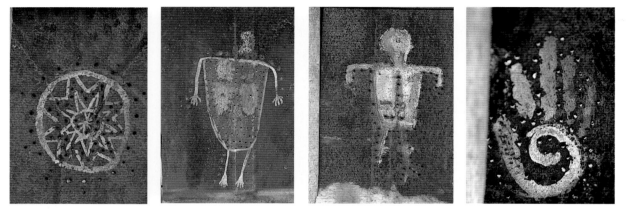

STRIPS OF OLD WOODEN LATTICE TAKE ON A STUNNING CHECKERBOARD EFFECT WHEN THEY ARE SEPARATED AND REVEAL THE UNEXPOSED SECTIONS OF WOOD. THE THIN WOOD, ALTHOUGH NOT STURDY ENOUGH FOR BIG PROJECTS, IS PERFECT TO USE IN SMALL ACCENT PIECES, SUCH AS PLANTERS AND DISPLAY BOXES. CREATE LUMINARIAS, AS DESIGNER JULIE ESCH DID, WITH CLEVER SPACING OF THE WOOD PIECES OR THE USE OF PUNCHED-OUT DESIGNS ON SALVAGED METAL WALLS.

"What are little girls made of? Rusty tin and old wood! I would watch my grandfather transform a dairy farmer's milk can into a bench and make a working lawn mower from old farm tools. It was crazy the stuff he came up with. And it was so neat—I grew up loving it."

—JULIE ESCH

MATERIALS

Salvaged lattice

Salvaged metal sheets, such as old tin roofing

White gesso (found in craft stores)

TOOLS

Pencil and paper

Wood nails and screws as needed

Handsaw

Tin snips

Power drill and wood screws as needed

Screwdriver

Hammer

Sandpaper

Center punch

Paintbrush

GENERAL INSTRUCTIONS

1 Julie, who isn't a professional woodworker, designed these wood projects on principles she already knew from her pottery training—the basic pottery shapes of body, foot, and lip. Look at the photos and you'll notice that each project is indeed divided into three separate parts. Plan your own designs on paper using the photos as guidance. Cut the pieces to match and apply the appropriate instructions as needed.

2 You're not making fine furniture here (just wonderfully clever decorative pieces) so you don't have to worry about fitting everything perfectly. Just glue and nail your pieces together. Use the photographs to guide you.

3 The body is basically a rectangular box attached to slender feet (or legs). Notice that, instead of making squat legs, Julie gave them height by cutting them at a 45° angle on the bottom. The rim holds the box and the leg-frame together, giving the structure a finished look. The rim is flush with the interior of the box and overhangs it on the outside. It's cut in standard 45° angles, just like a picture frame.

4 To add a striking, dramatic touch, Julie used salvage metal sheets as part of her basic box structure in three of the pieces. Fascinated by Native American rock art and petroglyphs, she added her version of ancient designs to the metal. Such prehistoric imagery, combined with the weathered grey of the wood, gives the pieces an aura of mystery.

5 Draw the image you like on the metal pieces, and then paint them with white gesso. If you want to make a luminaria, punch holes in the metal with the center punch. (See the photos to guide you.)

BOX WITH PAINTED MEN

Two sides are horizontal slats; two sides are metal. Measure, cut with the tin snips, and decorate the metal sides, punching holes with the center punch if you want light to shine through. Fold the bottom of the tin pieces 90° inward to create flat inside edges. Cut the legs and attach them firmly so the tin sides are held securely. Nail molding on  top of the tin sides, which will add support to the top and more security to the tin. Add the rim.

ALL-WOOD BOX

All the sides are made of wood, placed vertically and arranged to show off the lattice's old-paint checkerboard effect. First make the box including its sturdy base, then add the legs, leg braces, and the rim.

BOX WITH ROCK ART MAN AND SUN WITH ANTELOPE

Make a simple two-sided wooden box similar to the Box with Painted Men on page 76, except place the slats vertically to create a different design with the wood.

BOX WITH HAND

The two sides are horizontally placed lattice slats, the back is vertically placed slats, and the front combines vertically placed sections of barn wood and metal inserts. Leave large gaps between the vertical boards, so if you put a candle inside the box it will shine through the gaps. Add the tin in the center of the inside front, attach it, then strategically cover it with wood blocks.

STURDY METAL EDGING

Salvaged metal pieces, such as the metal roof rectangles Jeff salvaged from an old barn, make edging that is both wonderfully sturdy and versatile. It can be used for borders, terraces, raised beds, pathways, and any edge where you want to add curves.

DESIGN TIP

Notice how sensational the metal edging looks when rocks are included in the design of a terrace. The metal, plants, and rocks provide a wonderful variety of textures, colors, and shapes that all work beautifully together in the same space.

It's multiples that turn me on for salvage style art outdoors. If I find one great thing, I'm excited, but I don't always know what to do with that one. When I find 30 or 40 or 50 of something—ah ha! They start to grow with possibilities.

— "MR. JEFF" MENZER

MATERIALS

Flat salvaged exterior metal roofing rectangles:

> Small rectangles, 18 x 12 inches (45.7 x 30.5 cm), are old, and usually found in old barns or roofing sheets

> Larger rectangles, 8 x 2 feet (2.4 x .62 m), are newer and easier to find

1/8-inch (3 mm) diameter rebar, pre-cut to 18 inches (45.7 cm) long, as many as needed to stake the metal rectangles

Optional: metal bolts, railroad spikes, railroad support plates, and window sash weights or other heavy vertical pieces as extra support and visual variety

Marker

Work gloves and work boots

TOOLS

Measuring tape

Edging shovel or hand mattock

Sledge hammer

Heavy duty pliers

INSTRUCTIONS:
SMALL RECTANGLES

1 If you are making edging for terraces, start at the top terrace and work your way downhill. Measure how long you want your edging to stretch, and collect enough pieces to cover it, including the amount you'll need to overlap the pieces. (See step 4.)

2 With the edging shovel or small mattock, dig a small trench 2 inches (5 cm) deep to hold the bottom sections of the metal. Place the soil at the edge of the trench because you'll use it to backfill in step 5.

3 Work with one flat metal rectangle at a time. Measure and mark the top third section. Bend it over to make a rounded edge at the top. Press it flat with the hammer or step on it firmly while wearing heavy work boots. Repeat the process for each piece.

4 Start inserting the rectangles, working in sections of several feet at a time. Overlap the edges on each rectangle 2 to 3 inches (5 to 7.6 cm). Insert one of the rebar sections in front of every other rectangle. Use the hammer to pound in the rebar at least 12 inches (30.5 cm), so that the rebar prevents the metal pieces from becoming dislodged. Without this sturdy support, the metal pieces may drift downhill.

5 Backfill behind the edging with the soil and tamp it smooth and firm.

6 Use the pliers to firmly crimp the overlapped edges in the metal pieces so they stay even and don't become loose.

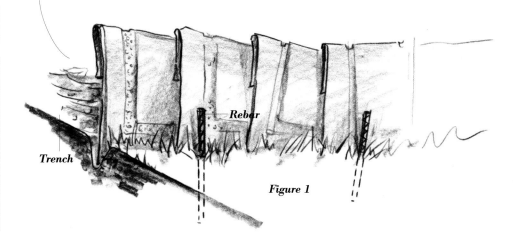

Backfill

Trench

Rebar

Figure 1

7 Check the edging annually for deterioration and soil erosion. Repair or replace any damaged metal and add soil, if necessary.

INSTRUCTIONS: LARGE RECTANGLES

1 Follow the same steps for the small rectangles with these changes: bend the panels in half lengthwise and overlap their edges 6 inches (15.2 cm) or more on each end.

2 Pre-bend the sections to help shape them if you want to create curves in the edging.

Bolts or railroad spikes at the bottom edge of the metal pieces add extra reinforcement and visual variety.

A cluster of big iron bolts makes a terrific decorative accent.

Above: To make edging with pretty glass bottles (blue and green are ideal) inserted upside down, follow the same instructions for edging with small metal rectangles with a few changes. Dig the trench deeper, at least 6 inches (15.2 cm). After backfilling, add river gravel or mulch along the front of the bottles to help keep them clean.

WELCOME ADDRESS POST

ANNOUNCE TO ALL YOUR VISITORS THAT THEY HAVE ARRIVED AT A HOUSE OF DISTINCTION! THIS CHEERY ADDRESS POST IS FUN TO MAKE AND EVEN MORE FUN TO COME HOME TO EACH DAY. TAKE OUR GENERAL DIRECTIONS AND DESIGN YOUR OWN VARIATION.

INSTRUCTIONS

1 Set the column securely on the workhorses. On the top of the column, measure and mark cutting lines so that the column ends in spear-shape, like a pitched roof. Cut with the saw.

2 Prepare the column with paint, stain, or preservative as you wish. The less you alter the wood, the more natural it will look. The more color you apply, the more cheerful it appears. Also, the more copper shapes on the post, the more interesting it is, even if the color is monochromatic. (If you are going to insert the column directly into the ground, coat the bottom with wood preservative will help it last longer.)

3 With the end of a copper nail, trace your house numbers on the copper sheets, keeping all the numbers the same size and style. Cut them out with the tin snips. Nail the numbers to the wood with the copper nails. If you wish, add windows made of slivered wood.

4 Cut any other copper details you want, such as decorative trim, and nail them to the post.

5 Measure and cut a rectangle of copper to make the roof. Using a dowel or your fingers, curve the side edges up for a whimsical touch. Fold the rectangle in half so that it creases at the ridgeline of the roof and place it on top of the column. Hold it steady while you nail it into the post.

6 See page 25 for posthole instructions and, with your helper, insert the post into the ground.

MATERIALS

One sturdy wood column or post (the one in the photo had been a porch column)

Flat copper sheet, salvaged

Wood preservative, paint, or stain (optional)

Copper nails as needed

Gravel

TOOLS

Pencil

Pair of workhorses

Tape measure

Circular saw or handsaw

Tin snips

Hammer

Dowel (optional)

Helper to assist inserting the post

I'm proud of my work with salvaged materials, and there's nothing like a beautiful front-yard project to share my enthusiasm with my neighbors.

– BRADLEY BARRETT

VICTORIAN CHICKADEE BIRDHOUSE

CHARM YOUR NEIGHBORS AND SHELTER YOUR FEATHERED FRIENDS WITH THIS DELIGHTFULLY CUCKOO SALVAGE-STYLE BIRDHOUSE. FOLLOW OUR GENERAL INSTRUCTIONS TO MAKE YOUR OWN VERSION, USING WHATEVER SALVAGE PIECES YOU FAVOR. TO ATTRACT CHICKADEES, PLACE THE BIRDHOUSE IN A WOODLAND CLEARING OR AT THE EDGE OF THE WOODS

"Salvage wood pieces give me more possibilities to be creative and spontaneous, and they already have character that new wood doesn't have. I love the history. Let's say I'm salvaging an old stairway, I wonder who walked on it..."

—ROLF HOLMQUIST

BASIC DIMENSIONS
FOR A BIRDHOUSE FOR CHICKADEES

Height above ground: 4 to 8 feet
(1.21 to 2.4 m)

Floor size: 4 x 4 inches
(101.6 x 101.6 mm)

Box Height: 11 to 13 inches
(279.4 to 330.2 mm)

Entrance above floor: 6 to 8 inches
(152.4 to 203.2 mm)

Entrance hole: $1^1/8$ inch (25.71 mm)
diameter

To attract nuthatchers, the entrance hole
should be bigger, between $1^1/4$ and $1^3/8$
inches (31.75 to 34.9 mm) in diameter

SALVAGE MATERIALS:
BIRDHOUSE BOX/ROOF/POST

2 2 x 4s for center supports, precut to 9
inches (228.6 mm) long

1 wood block for base, pre-cut to $1^1/2$ x 9 x 9
inches (38.1 x 228.6 x 228.6 mm)

1 wood block, for the internal floor, $4^1/4$ x
$3^1/2$ inches (109.5 x 88.9 mm)

2 salvaged doorjamb sections, for the front
and back of the birdhouse, pre-cut to 4 x 13
inches (101.6 x 330.2 mm) with a 45° angle
on their tops to fit under the roof

2 salvaged doorjamb sections, for the uneven
sides, precut to 7 inches (177.8 mm wide,
and 12 to 19 inches (304.8 to 482.6 mm)
long

2 window jambs or ornate table legs as front
decoration, precut to the same lengths as
the two side sections (or a bit longer for
dramatic effect)

Concrete medallion salvaged from an old
fireplace, 4 x 4 inches (101.6 x 101.6 mm)

2 pieces $3/4$-inch (19.05 mm) exterior plywood for the roof sofit, precut to 9 x 12
inches (228.6 x 304.8 mm)

Tin ceiling tile, about 2 feet x 15 inches
(609.6 x 381 mm)

2 small decorative "stairway" spindles, pre-
cut to fit under the roof eaves

2 salvaged wooden shelf brackets with fili-
gree, precut to fit as eaves

Part of a brass wall sconce or any other
metal salvage that looks like a bell hanging
over a door

Salvaged porch post, about 8 feet
(2.4 m) high

1 spring from an old screen door

SALVAGE MATERIALS:
STEEPLE/CUPOLA

1 wood block for the steeple base, precut
to $5^1/2$ x $3^1/2$ x 4 inches (139.7 x 88.9 x
101.6 mm)

1 picture frame for decoration, $5^1/2$ x
$3^1/2$ inches (139.7 x 88.9 mm) on outside edge of frame

$1/4$-inch (6 mm) base molding, precut to
fit around the picture frame

1 smaller wood block, 4 x $2^1/2$ x $3/4$ inch
(101.6 x 63.5 x 19 mm) as a layer on top
of the picture frame

1 decorative coffee table leg as the
steeple, about 10 inches (254 mm) long

1 brass doorknob for the top of the
steeple

OTHER MATERIALS

Bar soap to rub on the sofits

Galvanized screws and nails, $1^1/2$ inch
(38.1 mm)

All-weather wood glue

Exterior paint, color(s) of your choice

TOOLS

Saw, your choice

Hammer

Drill with $1^1/8$-inch (25.7 mm) drill bit

Galvanized nails or screws, as needed

Tin snips

Paintbrush

Post hole digger

INSTRUCTIONS:
BIRDHOUSE BODY AND ROOF

1 Precut the wood as indicated in the materials list on the opposite page, or according to your own design.

2 Set the wood block base at right angles to the wood for the front section, then measure and mark the wood from the top of the base to a point in the center, 6 to 8 inches (152.4 to 203.2 mm) above it. This is the entrance hole for the birdhouse. Drill it at a diameter of $1^1/8$ inch (25.7 mm).

3 Using the photo as a guide, glue and then nail or screw the wood pieces together. Basically you are making an open-topped box out of the pieces for the front, back, two sides, and the internal floor. To this box you'll later add decoration on the outside and a roof on the top.

■ Screw the 2 x 4s to one another to form the vertical central support

■ Screw the internal floor piece to the top of the 2 x 4s.

■ From the bottom of the internal floor piece, attach the precut front and back sections with the 45° tops.

■ Attach the precut side sections. Do so in a fashion that allows the

sections to run past the internal floor piece. This will add aesthetics and give the floor piece protection from weather damage by recessing it inside the birdhouse walls.

4 Add the window jambs or ornate table legs as decorative pieces on the front.

5 Attach the concrete medallion to the bottom of the front section so that it covers the internal floor piece, adding further protection from the weather.

6 Rub the inside of the exterior plywood pieces with bar soap to prevent hornets and bees from making their nests inside the birdhouse. Then attach the pieces to form the roof sofits. You've now enclosed the birdhouse box.

7 Bend the salvaged ceiling tin into a 45° angle and nail it to the sofit.

8 Nail the stairway spindles underneath the center of the roof in both the front and back of the birdhouse.

9 Nail the wooden shelf brackets at each end of the tin roof on the front.

INSTRUCTIONS:
STEEPLE/CUPOLA

10 Cut a "V" into the steeple base block of wood so that it straddles the 45° roof. Center and attach the base to the tin roof.

11 About $1/2$ inch (12.7 mm) down from the top of the steeple base, fit the picture frame around its sides and attach it. Glue the base molding around the underside of the picture frame for ornamentation.

12 Attach the smaller block of wood on top of the picture frame and molding to create a layered look.

13 Attach the precut coffee table leg on top of the steeple base.

14 Attach the doorknob to the top of the steeple.

15 Attach the brass wall sconce to the stairway spindle underneath

the eave on the front. It should jut past the birdhouse from the apex of the roof.

16 Attach the screen door spring to one side of the birdhouse, just under the overhanging roof.

17 Paint with exterior paint in the color of your choice. Let it dry, then sand the paint to give a weathered look.

18 You've finished the birdhouse! You can keep the birdhouse indoors as an art piece. Or attach it to the sturdy post and display it outside. If you do display it, attach another set of small spindle railings, cut to size, between the base of the bird-house and the post. (See the photo on page 85.) See the posthole digging instructions on page 25.

BIRDFEEDER INSTRUCTIONS

Assemble the roof in a similar manner to the birdhouse roof, using whatever salvage materials you have. The tray is an old draw-er with a bottom of 3/4-inch (19.05 mm) exterior plywood, such as you used for the birdhouse sofits. The tray must be smaller than the roof so the roof can overhang it and keep the seeds dry. Make the feeder porch legs out of mismatched chair legs cut to the same height. In each corner of the bottom part of the tray, drill some holes to let water drain out. Decorate as you wish with salvaged parts, and paint in the color of your choice.

VINTAGE HEAT REGISTER DOORMAT

VINTAGE HEAT REGISTERS WITH SIMPLE DESIGNS ARE READILY AVAILABLE AND STILL AFFORDABLE. HERE'S AN EASY PROJECT THAT PROVES PLAIN IS PRETTY.

MATERIALS

Metal vent or heat register cover

Lengths of salvaged wood that are thick enough to form a frame around the metal

Rust-preventing spray paint in your choice of color

Nails or wood screws as needed

Wood preservative

Good quality exterior oil-based stain

TOOLS

Wire brush

Orbital sander or sandpaper

Rag or paintbrush for the stain

Rubber-headed mallet, if needed

INSTRUCTIONS

1 Brush off loose debris from the heat register. Paint it as many colors as you like, drying and sanding between coats. To achieve a warm weathered look, use two coats—orange, then red. Sand the corners and other raised areas to reveal the colors in the undercoats, as if many years of use have exposed the paint layers.

2 Measure the underside of the grate, the part that would have dropped in to the floor, then cut four lengths of the wood to fit snugly, mitering them at 45° angles. Nail or screw the frame together.

3 Seal the wood with wood preservative. When dry, use the rag or paintbrush to stain the wood the color you want. Wipe off any excess stain and let it dry completely.

4 Drop the painted grate into the frame. It may be a tight fit—if needed, use the mallet to gently pound it into place.

FIREWOOD RACK WITH PIPE PORTHOLES

ROUND PIPES INSERTED AMONG THE SHARP, HARD-EDGED PIECES OF CUT WOOD TRANSFORM AN ORDINARY FIREWOOD STORAGE RACK INTO A THING OF BEAUTY.

MATERIALS

Wood and kindling cut to fit your fireplace

Sections of big pipe in any material you can salvage, including metal or concrete culverts, plastic sewer lines, or industrial piping

Sturdy metal firewood holder with sides (find one at a home improvement center, or make one)

TOOLS

Cutting tools appropriate to the material of the pipes, such as a circular saw for plastic, a reciprocating saw with a metal cutting blade for metal, or a masonry circular saw for concrete

File and grinding tools appropriate to the material of the pipe

INSTRUCTIONS

1 Find or cut sections of pipe to the same length as the average piece of your firewood, usually 2 to 3 feet (.61 to .9 m) long and 18 inches (45.7 cm) or more in diameter. Use slightly different diameters for variety.

2 File or grind smooth any sharp points and edges on the pipe sections.

3 As you neatly stack the pieces of firewood into the rack, fit the pipe sections among them.

4 Stack kindling into the pipes, leaving the tops empty so you can see through them as if they are portholes to the other side of the garden.

Advice on salvage style for the garden? Don't worry about being perfect.

–"Mr. Jeff" Menzer

GRATE STEPPINGSTONES

Y OU'LL REALLY BE WALKING THROUGH YOUR GARDEN IN STYLE IF YOU PLACE THESE SENSATIONAL STEPPINGSTONES IN YOUR PATH. THE NON-SLIPPERY CENTERS ARE VINTAGE HEATING GRATES, RESTING IN CONCRETE BASES MADE IN SIMPLE, ADJUSTABLE FORMS AND PAINTED LOVELY COLORS. WHAT A GRATE IDEA!

I tend to pick a lot of things up, and I have no idea what I am going to do with them. I picked up a piece of metal grating off the street —and you know how the creative process works—I was standing there brushing my teeth and suddenly I knew what to do with the grate. That piece was the inspiration for the whole project.

—LAURIE CORRAL

MATERIALS

4 1 x 6 plank boards, 12 inches (3.5 cm) long

Salvaged heating grates

4 standard metal L-brackets, 2 x 2 inches (5 x 5 cm)

Concrete mix, the type with fiberglass threads (The concrete mix with fiberglass threads is more expensive than the standard mix, but it gives the concrete much more strength, which is advisable for steppingstones.)

Large heavy trash bag

Bag of potter's clay

Latex (or rubber) gloves

Round 4-gallon (18.9 L) bucket

Water source

Sponges

Acrylic paint with good pigment density, color of your choice

Clear acrylic protective coating for concrete (optional)

TOOLS

Marker

Garden trowel

Screwdriver

Power drill with small paint mixer attachment

Soft cleaning brush

Paintbrush (optional)

INSTRUCTIONS

1 To make a non-porous bottom for your frame, place the garbage bag or heavy plastic on a level surface and set your heating grate on top of it.

2 Fit the plank boards of the form together to make a border 2 to 3-inches (5 to 7.6 cm) out from the edges of the grate.

3 After you've decided if you want the shutters open or closed (see Choose the Look of Each Steppingstone on page 94) measure the height your grate will reach, and mark the spot on the inside of the plank board forms. This will be the approximate depth to pour the concrete. Remove the grate and set it aside for now.

4 Roll a little bit of damp potter's clay in your hands to make pencil-width coils and use them to seal the corners and bottom edges of the form. The clay will stay moist for a few hours, but not overnight. So be sure to pour the concrete before the clay dries to prevent the seals from shrinking and cracking.

HOW TO MAKE AN ADJUSTABLE FORM FOR CONCRETE

Screw in one of the L-brackets on the end of each plank board. (See the illustration.) The brackets should extend beyond the length of the boards by one board-width or approximately 1 inch (2.5 cm). You'll be able to adjust the boards of the form to fit the sizes and shapes (square or rectangular) of all your grates.

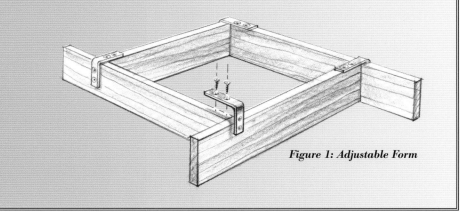

Figure 1: Adjustable Form

DESIGN TIP

OLDER HEATING GRATES ARE MORE DECORATIVE THAN NEW ONES, BUT THEY ARE EXPENSIVE AND HARDER TO FIND. IF YOU CAN FIND SEVERAL AT A REASONABLE COST, GRAB THEM. BUT DON'T TURN AWAY FROM THE NEWER, PLAINER DESIGNS. THEY ARE MUCH MORE AFFORDABLE, AND THERE ARE ENOUGH VARIATIONS IN THEIR GRIDS TO WORK QUITE WELL IN A GROUPING.

6 Set out the electric drill and its mixer attachment, the bucket, garden trowel, water source, and your protective gloves. Following the concrete manufacturer's directions, mix enough concrete in the bucket to fill the form to the marks you made in step 3. (Usually 4 to 6 trowels of cement should do it.) The proper consistency is like pudding. Don't panic if you don't have enough concrete to reach the mark—you can mix and add more in the next step.

7 Push the grate into the concrete until it rests on the plastic. The top of the grate should be level with or slightly above the surface of the concrete. Pour more mix if necessary.

8 Sponge off any excess concrete that flows over onto the surface of the grate.

9 Follow the concrete manufacturer's instructions, and let the concrete set for 36 to 48 hours.

10 Wipe or brush off any excess concrete again.

11 Mix acrylic paints and swipe them into the surface of the steppingstone. Laurie used bright colors such as burnt sienna, green-gold, cobalt blue, white, and red-violet, which will weather nicely. Make washes of the colors, layer and blend them freely, using several colors on each stone. Allow the paint to dry completely.

12 Finish the stepping-stones with a clear protective coating made especially for concrete surfaces. Eventually a beautiful natural patina will develop.

13 Bury the stones so their tops are level with the ground sur-

face. If you place them in a grassy area, make sure they are deep enough to easily clear the blades of a lawn mower. They also look terrific in pathways of pea gravel or wood chips.

CHOOSE THE LOOK OF EACH STEPPING-STONE

If the shutters are open in the grate, the grate will be taller in the bed of concrete, and you'll need more concrete to fill in the spaces between the open shutters and smoothly match their height. The stone will be thick and heavy.

If the shutters in the grate are closed, the grate will be lower in the bed of concrete—a steppingstone that is thinner and lighter in weight.

Whether the shutters are open or closed, the weight of the grate will cause it to come to rest at the bottom of the form on top of the plastic.

PIPE WAVE FENCE

Design
"MR. JEFF" MENZER

ALMOST EVERYTHING ABOUT THIS EVOCATIVE FENCE WAS SALVAGED, INCLUDING THE GENTLY CURVED BRANCHES FROM A FELLED WHITE BIRCH. THE DESIGN IS REMARKABLY SIMPLE: A SERIES OF METAL ARCHES LINKED TOGETHER IN A THREE TO ONE RATIO, WITH THE TREE LIMBS ATTACHED LIKE FENCE PICKETS.

MATERIALS

For the fence arches: Any metal piping that is rusty, long, and thin. The fence in the photo is 80 feet (24 m) long and 10 feet (3 m) high. The designer used twelve pieces of salvaged steel water pipes which are 1 inch (2.5 cm) in diameter and 20 feet (6.1 m) long. Each one weighs about 40 pounds (18 k).

For the arch supports: For each arch you'll need two pieces of rebar narrower than the arch pipes. The fence in the photo used twenty-four pieces of rebar, $1/4$ to $1/2$ inch (6 mm to 1.3 cm) in diameter, pre-cut to 36 inches (.91m) in length

For the fence pickets: Trimmed tree limbs, 3 to 10 feet (.9 to 3 m) long, diameter about as big as your wrist, 2 to 4 inches (5 to 10.2 cm). The number of limbs depends on the length of your fence and how closely you want them spaced. The designer chose birch tree limbs because of their lovely paleness and their curved shapes.

For the lashings: Zinc-coated steel wire, 18 gauge (If you want the wire to be noticed, use copper or colored wire.)

TOOLS

Guide wire or rope

Protective gloves

Tree trimming tools such as lopers, pruning saw, and hand pruners

Old towels or other padding

Sledgehammer

Lineman's pliers

Hand sledge

Wire cutters

Helper, strong and able to carry and lift, needed throughout

LOCATION

Near the fence site you'll need two sturdy trees that are close together, about 2 to 3 feet (.61 to .9 m) apart. You'll use these trees to curve the metal pipes into arches in step 1.

BEFORE YOU START

Collect all the materials and bring them to the site. Arrange the materials so you can gather them easily and work safely.

Measure and lay out your fence line with wire or rope as a guide to keep the fence straight.

With the appropriate trimming tools, trim the side branches off the tree limbs, leaving the branches as clean as possible. Check for the sturdiness of the limbs, especially if they have been stored outside for a while. Rock the limb back and forth over your knee. A healthy limb will bend; one with dry rot will break. Don't use any pieces that have dry rot because they won't last.

INSTRUCTIONS

1 Using the old towels, pad the trunks of the two nearby trees. With you on one end of the pipe and your helper on the other, place the steel pipe into an S-shape around the front of one tree and the back of the other. Then push and pull the pipe until you achieve a long, gentle curve in the middle of the pipe. (See the photo on page 95 and fig. 1 on page 97 for guidance.) Keep 3 feet (.9 m) on each end of the pipe unbent because that's the part of the pipe you'll insert over the rebar in step 2. Shape all the arch pipes and set them aside.

2 Start the fence at one end. With the sledgehammer, drive one of the rebar supports halfway into the ground at a steep (about 45°) angle. With your helper, slide the end of one of the arch pipes over the rebar.

3 With your helper, bend the steel arch pipe over in a smooth half-circle until it touches the ground in a straight axis down the fence line. You want the top of the circle to be no higher than about 6 feet (1.8 m) tall so you can lash the branches to the pipe later. Mark the spot where the pipe touches the ground—then move the marker about a foot (30.5 cm)

closer and drive in the other rebar support here. (Shortening the distance between the supports will increase the curve of the arch pipe.) Slide the opposite end of the arch pipe over the second rebar. (It will take some strength to do this.) You've now completed one arch of the fence with two rebar supports at either end.

4 To place the second arch, repeat steps 2 and 3, starting this arch one-third of the distance between the ends of the first arch. Use the wire to lash the arches together where they cross.

5 Start the third arch two-thirds of the distance between the ends of the first arch. But instead of driving the rebar support on the same axis line as the previously placed rebars, drive this rebar support slightly

behind, so that it is about the diameter of an arch pipe behind the first and second arches. (Placing the arches in front and behind one another increases the sturdiness of the fence and keeps it on a straight line.) Repeat steps 2 to 4, lashing the pipes firmly where they cross.

6 Continue to add the arches at one-third intervals, alternating them front and back from the previous arch until the row of arches is completed.

7 To complete the feel of movement in the fence, you'll want to have the birch limbs go all the way to the end. Place an additional arch underneath the last arch, thus giving the last tree limbs two spots in which to be lashed.

8 Go take a rest and come back tomorrow!

9 On the ground in front of the metal arches, lay out your

Use 18 gauge wire to lash each tree limb to its metal pipe arch.

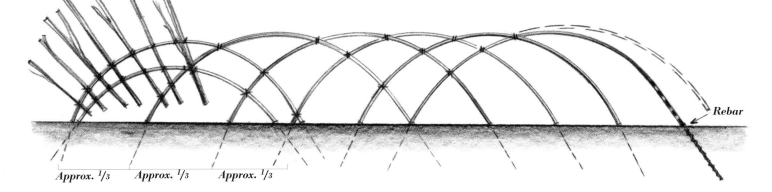

Rebar

Approx. 1/3   Approx. 1/3   Approx. 1/3

Figure 1

Jeff made a simple yet serviceable fence that also has a natural look by crisscrossing salvaged rebar and straight wooden poles.

trimmed birch limb pickets to make a pleasing pattern. To replicate the fence in the photo, place shorter pieces at each end and the longest pieces radiating like waves throughout the middle, each limb curving elegantly in the same direction.

10 Starting in the middle with your longest branches, lash the limbs to the arches. Keep each limb about 12 inches (30.5 cm) above ground to avoid decay, and lash it in two or more places with the wire. Keep your lashings consistent and they'll disappear from sight. As you continue to lash all the limbs, keep checking to make sure that they are evenly spaced.

11 Tuck in all the wires, watching for sharp points. Use the wire cutters to trim the ends, and bend them down for safety. If you want, cover the steel wire lashings with organic material such as hemp or rope.

In many projects you have the idea for the project first— and then you look for materials. I find the opposite in working with salvage: first you find the materials and then you imagine a potential use for it. It's a whole different mindset. I had seen that steel pipe at the salvage yard at least ten times, and finally I said "What can I do with this?"

—"Mr. Jeff" Menzer

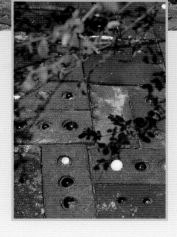

The old piano frame is too heavy to turn into a fence and too beautiful to hide under plants as a trellis—so why not show it off in your front yard for the whole neighborhood to enjoy?

Old marbles in old bricks make colorful new walkways.

Several kinds of salvaged edging give variety to a garden.

ALL DESIGNS BY "MR. JEFF" MENZER

A screen of vintage shutters is made steady with simple wooden supports.
COURTESY OF RHONDA AND WAYNE WILLIAMS, WOODFIELD INN

A tabletop shrine of salvaged wood filled with treasured mementos makes a priceless gift.
DESIGN BY CHARLES MURRAY

An ornate old ceiling fixture takes on new light as a candleholder.
DESIGN BY BUNNY DARR

Show off your old hardware and crystals on a screen made from salvaged rebar.
DESIGN BY BRADLEY BARRETT

Antique bricks from Cotswold stone make a unique bench that's hard—but oh, so beautiful!
COURTESY OF MINCHINHAMPTON ARCHITECTURAL SALVAGE COMPANY

When streets are torn up to be repaired, you can often find concrete or old granite curbing to salvage and transform into magnificent benches.

From eighteenth-century farms come perfectly modern garden sculptures—a staddle stone and a trough to fill with flowers.
COURTESY OF UNIQUITIES ARCHITECTURAL ANTIQUES

Stone cut in the nineteenth century is salvaged into a modern outdoor dining suite.
DESIGN AND PHOTO BY JAMES CHRISTOPHER SITTIG

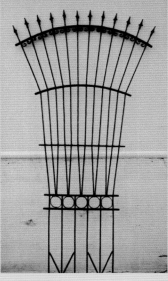

Keep climbing plants pruned in
order to show off the fine lines of
a trellis such as this one, made
from various fence parts.
DESIGN BY BRAD OLIVER

Salvaged tin tile roofing, rebar, and copper wire work together
beautifully in this three-legged chair. DESIGN BY CYNTHIA WYNN

An elaborate salvage style birdhouse, based on an
old church design, is made for chickadees.
DESIGN BY ROLF HOLMQUIST

Cutouts made with a plasma cutter give this salvaged metal bench
its fanciful look.
CUTOUT DESIGN BY GRACE CATHEY

It's almost a shame to cover this distinctive salvaged
steel rebar bench with seat cushions.
DESIGN BY BRAD OLIVER

Little salvage style birdhouses make sweet garden accents.
DESIGN BY SIMONE WILSON

This brightly colored birdhouse, constructed of salvaged wood and metal pieces, is designed to house happy house wrens, tufted titmice, or chickadees.
DESIGN BY SIMONE WILSON

This long, sturdy display bench was made from cast-off check plate and big hollow metal pipes found in a scrap yard.
DESIGN BY CHRISTOPHER D. MELLO

A metal fruit barrel is cut and then brightly painted to become a stylish planter.
DESIGN BY ANNE KAUFMANN

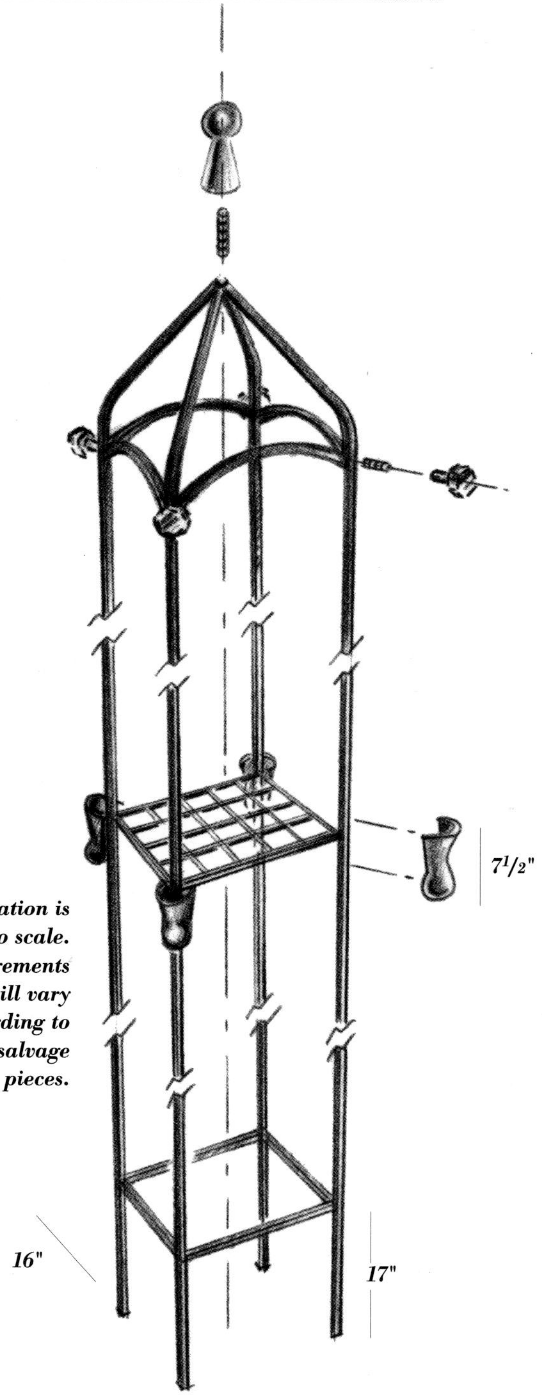

Illustration is
not to scale.
Measurements
will vary
according to
your salvage
pieces.

7½"

16"

17"

Figure 1

GARDEN GODDESS TRELLIS

THREE YEARS AGO, DESIGNER DANA IRWIN BOUGHT A
BEAUTIFUL CAST-IRON GRATE FEATURING THE IMAGE OF
A WOMAN TENDING A FIRE—PERHAPS THE GODDESS HESTIA,
PATRONESS OF THE HEARTH. AS OFTEN HAPPENS WITH SALVAGE
PIECES, IT SAT AND WAITED. ONCE SHE WAS INSPIRED TO TURN
THE GRATE INTO THE CENTERPIECE OF A SMALL TRELLIS, DANA
QUICKLY DREW A SKETCH AND STARTED LOOKING FOR OTHER
SALVAGE PARTS. WELDER/FABRICATOR LARRY FREER TURNED
HER IDEAS INTO THIS MAGICAL LANDSCAPE SCULPTURE. USE OUR
GENERAL INSTRUCTIONS AS A GUIDE AND MAKE YOUR OWN DESIGN.

*The joy of putting this project together was the idea of being able to
see the beautiful grate appreciated at eye level. Finding the other
pieces took time, but it was fun, and as I found the different pieces,
they helped define the specifics of the design.*

—DANA M. IRWIN

The most important thing salvage style design-ers need to remember is: maybe you don't weld, but somebody else does. You just need to get the two of you together.

—LARRY FREER

MATERIALS

Cast iron gate with figure design

Two legs from a clawfoot tub for candle holders

Metal figure of a lion's paw holding a crystal ball for decorative top

Four glass drawer knobs as decoration to hide weld joints

Metal grate for shelf

Square-sided rods, $^1/_2$ inch (1.3 cm) in diameter, cut to length, as the frame

Paper, pencil and tape measure

TOOLS

Welder's tools:

Electric arc welder

Oxy/acetylene torch

Bench vise

Chop saw or hacksaw

Welding gloves

Pliers

GENERAL INSTRUCTIONS

1 Gather all your pieces. Draw your design and write in exact measurements. Seek recommendations for a welder/fabricator from friends who've had welding done. Then get estimates from several professionals. (See Working with a Welder/Fabricator: Advice from a Pro on page 22.)

2 Once you find the welder/fabricator you like, talk over the project with him or her. For example, after Larry looked at Dana's designs, he advised increasing the length of the legs 4 inches (10.2 cm) so the trellis would be more stable. Larry suggested Dana might want to use round-edged rods instead of square ones— but she remained adamant and Larry complied. They both agreed to use glass for the shelf so that nothing would distract from the cast iron grate figure. But later, after the glass broke when placed against its metal supports, they agreed that even thick glass was too risky for such an open design. Dana decided to find a simple metal grate as a shelf and have it welded in at a later date.

3 Larry's main concern was not that Dana's artistic design would be difficult to weld, but that it had two types of metal, meaning he would have to weld dissimilar metals. Because he's an experienced welder, Larry knew what filler metal and rod to use. A beginning welder might not have been able to do this job.

MARVELOUS MELLO FOUNTAIN

Y OU NEED TO BE AN INTREPID SALVAGER TO FIND THE ROUNDED SAL-VAGED STEEL PIECES FOR THIS FOUNTAIN. BUT GUESS WHAT? THE ENTIRE MARVELOUS WONDER IS PUT TOGETHER WITHOUT ANY WELDING, SO EVEN A BRASH SALVAGE BEGINNER CAN MAKE SOMETHING SIMILAR.

Bonnie-Mae and Belle love to play in the water that is always freshly recirculated in this easy-to-make fountain.

One of the things I love about this project is that it is modular. I could really disassemble it and move it with relatively little effort. With shims on top of the legs, you can reduce or deepen the amount of water in the plates. It's all so easy!

— CHRISTOPHER D. MELLO

MATERIALS

2 (or more, depends on how grandiose you want to get!) curved steel pieces at least ¼ inch (6 mm) thick

Plastic bowl to hold the pump

Salvaged metal or concrete blocks or anything that is sturdy enough to serve as legs to hold up the metal plates

Low-HP recirculating pump (It's amazing how much water these little guys pump out!)

GFCI (ground fault circuit interrupter)

Gravel and dirt, as needed

TOOLS

Shovel, as needed

Grinder to grind smooth the edges of the metal pieces, if needed

ABOUT SCRAP YARD METAL FOUNTAINS

The challenge with this project is to find steel salvage pieces that are already concave enough to hold water. If you're familiar with the joys of scrap yard hunting, you're bound to find some. The pieces Christopher found were from an old water tower that had deteriorated in his neighborhood.

Both steel pieces were about ¼ inch (6 mm) thick. The top base is about 4 x 4 feet (1.21 x 1.21 m) and the one below it is about 3½ x 2 feet (1.06 x .6 m). You can use any size you want as long as the one on top is a little wider than the one below. (Or not! There's no rule about it!) If needed, grind the edges of the salvage metal smooth.

A big plastic bowl is out of sight underneath the bottom piece of metal. This bowl holds the recirculating pump, the kind of pump you'd use in ordinary garden fountains. You don't need a big powerful one. A small one will do just fine.

The way your bottom bowl fits in the configuration you create, and the depth of the water in the bowl, determines what kind of sound it makes. Christopher wanted the specific sound that comes from the water trickling into the plastic. But you could have a bottom bowl made of any kind of material, another steel piece, or ceramic, for example.

Anytime you have water and electricity in the garden, you need to take safety precautions. Here's where the GFCI comes in. If you should break the electric cord with a shovel, for example, the GFCI automatically shuts off the current and you'll be

safe. Have a qualified electrician install the GFCI and then you don't have to worry about it.

Christopher calls his garden the place where Dr. Seuss and Edward Gorey meet to have tea! He first lays down weed-preventing cloth then covers it with gravel. Then he places his edging, in this case, teeth from old bulldozers and backhoes. Salvage metal makes great foundations for outdoor art, such as for the clay sphere made by Robin Van Valkenburgh.

Long sections of giant chains create another unique landscape edging. Notice the sturdy salvage metal foundation that holds the big clay platter made by Mark Burleson. The enigmatic hand was made by O. David Vance.

Christopher's garden is bursting with all kinds of rare flowers. Here's a rusty spike flower made by Cynthia Wynn. (See the chair she made on page 102)

1 Position your lowest bowl and the pump in the fountain location.

2 Create the base for the bottom metal plate. Position salvaged metal "legs" as Christopher did or devise your own. Build up a nice pile of earth as the background, as if the fountain is coming out of a little mountain.

3 Put another set of legs on top of the bottom metal piece to hold the top piece and position it.

4 Set decorative pieces on the fountain as you wish, such as how Christopher displays his clay art. Fluff up the landscaping so all the mechanics are hidden.

5 Turn on the water and enjoy!

DESIGN TIP

MOVING WATER DOESN'T ATTRACT BUGS, SO YOU DON'T HAVE TO WORRY ABOUT THAT. BUT IF THE FOUNTAIN SHOULD STOP RUNNING, BUGS WILL MAKE THEMSELVES AT HOME VERY QUICKLY, SO USE A MOSQUITO REPELLANT WHEN NEEDED.

NATURE LOVERS GARDEN SHRINE

With skill and an appreciation for detail, designers Kitty Brown and Michael Mooney transform an old window frame and other cast-off pieces of salvage into a personal garden shrine. It sits conveniently at eye level, so they can just open the door and place sacred offerings safely inside.

May we all participate joyfully in the process of creation in the garden and become as nature itself through our endeavors.

— KITTY BROWN & MICHAEL MOONEY

MATERIALS

Salvaged wooden window frame with glass panes (3 panes is ideal)

4 pieces of weathered 1 x 6 wood, cut to length, for the sides of the box

Weathered pieces of 1 x10 wood, cut to length, for the back of the box

Newell post or similar large decorative post, at least 4 feet (1.2 m) high

Weatherproof wood glue

$1^1/_2$-inch (3.8 cm) trim screws, as needed, to make the box

$2^1/_4$-inch (5.7 cm) trim screws to attach the shrine box to the post

Bits of tile, glass, marbles, and dishes for the mosaic back

2 large hinges

Old drawer or cabinet knob

Hasp

Mastic

TOOLS

All-purpose cleaner and water

Stiff bristle brush

Measuring tape

Circular saw or chop saw

Hammer

Power drill with drill/screwdriver w/square drive bit

Gloves

Trowel for applying mastic

Helper needed to lift and move the post

INSTRUCTIONS

1 Clean the window frame with the cleaner and water, using the brush to remove any loose paint. Paint it if you wish, or leave it naturally weathered as the designers did.

2 With the 1 x 6 wood pieces, make a four-sided open box that will fit the window frame, butt-joined at each corner. Use the wood glue and the shorter screws to attach the pieces.

3 With the pieces of 1 x 10, make the back of the box, attaching the pieces with glue and screwing them into place on the box.

4 Because the mosaic back will make the shrine heavy and prone to damage, it's best to attach it to the post now, and do the mosaic work in the next step. If it's not already flat, cut off the top of the newel post. Apply glue to the bottom of the shrine and then use the $2^1/_4$-inch (5.7 cm) screws to attach its bottom to the post. With your helper's assistance, put the shrine upright, and let it dry for at least four hours. (If you wish, you can actually place the post in its permanent place now—see step 7.)

5 Make the decorative mosaic on the inside back, using salvaged pieces of tile-glass, and dishes. With the trowel, smear a coat of mastic about $1/_8$ to $1/_4$ inch (3 to 6 mm) thick to the inside back. With the tip of a screw, scratch your design lightly into the mastic surface. Apply the mosaic bits. (Look at the photos to see how pieces of cups and saucers were made into small shelves.) Allow a bit of mastic to well up between the mosaic pieces. Fill in with tile pieces close to the dish shards to help hold them up. Let dry for 24 hours.

6 Clean the windowpanes as necessary. Screw in the hinges to attach the window frame to the shrine. Attach the doorknob and the hasp to the door.

7 See the information on postholes on page 25 in the basics section and insert the shrine and its post into the ground. Bless the shrine and display things you love in it.

MAJESTIC BEADBOARD COLUMNS

With its distinctive thin, vertical stripes, beadboard is an ideal salvaged material to use when creating landscape columns. Adapt designer Jeff Burgner's general instructions to make columns suitable for your garden.

MATERIALS

Beadboard panels, cut into four matching lengths

3/4-inch (19.05 mm) pieces of barn wood (or similar wood), each cut to 8 inches (203.2 mm) wider than the width of your box to create an overhang

Large crown molding, cut as needed

Baseboard, cut as needed

Shoe molding, cut as needed

Nails and wood screws, as needed

Paint, stain, and/or wood preservative (optional)

TOOLS

Circular saw

Hammer

Sander or sandpaper

Helper as needed

BEFORE YOU START

After you read the instructions below, plan your design on paper so you know the measurements of your columns, what types of wood you'll need, and what colors and shapes you want to incorporate. With the circular saw, cut all the pieces of wood to your desired widths and lengths.

INSTRUCTIONS

1 Make a simple four-sided hollow box out of the beadboard by butting the corner joints together and nailing them.

2 Nail the pieces of barn wood to the top of the box, being careful to keep the 4-inch (101.6 mm) overhang even on all sides.

3 Add any trim you want to the top. The columns in the photo have large crown molding, which was mitered at each corner.

4 Add any trim you want to the bottom. You can nail baseboard directly to the frame and add shoe molding on top of it.

5 Sand and/or paint, and apply preservative as desired.

Whether perched on top of stately columns or nestled in greenery, salvaged concrete figures always add a classical touch to the garden.

MOSAIC GARDEN PANELS

S ALVAGED PIECES OF TILE, GLASS, AND MIRROR BECOME MOSAICS IN A PAIR OF GRAND GARDEN WALL PANELS. AT NIGHT, MIRROR PIECES REFLECT THE LIGHT FROM CANDLES PLACED ON THE SALVAGED SOAPHOLDERS. BY DAY, THEY CAPTURE THE SUN.

MATERIALS

Salvaged treated lumber, pre-cut to frame the plywood panels

$2^3/_4$-inch (1.9 cm) plywood panels, cut to your desired size

Salvaged pieces of tile, stained glass, and mirror

Salvaged soapholders or some other shelving device

Freeze/thaw stable mastic (outside projects need to withstand extreme weather changes)

Sanded grout, color of your choice

Terrycloth rags

De-hazer (found in tile stores)

Wood primer and outdoor paint to finish the backsides

TOOLS

$^3/_{16}$-inch (4.7 mm) notched trowel to spread the mastic

Hammer or tile nippers to control the shaping of your tile

Tiler's float or large stiff sponge

INSTRUCTIONS

1 Miter cut and nail four pieces of the salvaged lumber onto the back of the plywood panel to make a frame for it.

2 Place the plywood panel on a flat work surface and draw your design on it. (Notice the birds-of-paradise—Jessica used the panels in her wedding, so she included her wedding flowers in the design.) Plan the spacing

of your mirror pieces to maximize the reflection of the candlelight.

3 With the notched trowel, apply mastic to the plywood where you want to place the soapholders. Press them in and lightly swivel them a bit to get them fully into the mastic. Follow the mastic manufacturer's directions and let everything dry completely, at least 24 hours.

4 Applying mastic as needed, attach the parts of your design that are the most complicated, such as any flower stems and blossoms. Let them set completely.

5 Start the in-fill, applying small areas of the mastic with the trowel. For larger tile pieces, spread larger areas of mastic. Place fill color tile onto these areas. (It may be difficult to fit the trowel into some small areas—you'll need to mastic and place each piece individually.) Continue until the entire front of the panel is covered with tile.

6 Now it's time to grout the tiles. Following the manufacturer's instructions, and for the best and easiest application, keep the grout consistency like sandy cake batter. Spill at least 2 cups (.47 L) of mixed grout on the project. Use the tiler's float to push the grout into the grout lines in a small area, making sure you smooth out any air pockets that may have formed in the

grout. Hold the float level to the fill the grout lines; hold it at a 45° angle to remove excess grout.

7 Once the lines are filled in a small area, angle the float about 45° degrees and spread the grout (as if you were using a squeegee) to other parts of the project, adding more grout as needed until all the lines are full. Remove as much excess grout as possible with the float and allow the grout to dry for a bit until the tiles appear dusty or hazy.

8 Remove the grout haze with the terrycloth towel. (Be careful!) Leave them alone for a few minutes and if they appear clean, this part of the job is done. However, unfinished and textured tiles will require more attention. If your grout discolors these tiles, use a damp towel to carefully rub the individual surfaces. If there is still a haze after the grout is set, use the de-hazer to clean the whole project.

9 Paint the frame and the back of the plywood panel.

10 Repeat all the steps for the second panel.

11 Attach the panels to a wall or fence. Decorate the soapholders with candles, plants, or other decorative treasures. Stand back and admire your work!

HOW TO MAKE STAND-ALONE PANELS

As you can imagine, the panels are quite heavy, so if you want them to stand up in the garden by themselves (such as in the photo) you'll have to devise sturdy supports for them. Here's one way. For each panel, measure and cut two treated 2 x 4s so they will be long enough to attach to the top of the frame and extend to the ground. Pre-drill holes at an angle at the top of the 2 x 4s for long wood screws (the size depends on the thickness of your frame) and a $3/4$-inch (1.9 cm) hole near the bottom. Use sturdy wood screws to toenail the 2 x 4s to the top of the panel frame. Then, using a sledgehammer, drive 3-foot (.9 m) lengths of $1/2$-inch (1.3 cm) rebar through the bottom holes and into the ground.

SAFETY TIP

Be very careful not to cut yourself on the sharp edges of the pieces of tile and glass. Take care in every step of the mosaic process, from placing the pieces to cleaning them. Voice of Experience!

SPECIAL OCCASION PERGOLA

I MAGINE DESIGNER SIMON WHITELEY'S DELIGHT WHEN SOMEONE GAVE HIM SIX OLD COLUMNS, EACH 10 FEET (3 M) TALL. THE COLUMNS WERE ACTUALLY SOLID TREE TRUNKS, BORED ALL THE WAY THROUGH THE CENTER. SALVAGE TREASURES THIS WONDERFUL DON'T COME ALONG VERY OFTEN, SO SIMON WANTED TO MAKE SOMETHING SPECTACULAR OUT OF THEM, BUT DIDN'T HAVE THE SPACE FOR A PERMANENT STRUCTURE. WHY NOT MAKE SOMETHING TEMPORARY THAT COULD BE FAIRLY EASILY ERECTED FOR SPECIAL OCCASIONS AND BROKEN DOWN FOR EASY STORAGE? WHY NOT!

You never know where or when you'll find great salvage pieces. I bought the lumber as waste from a new construction site years ago, but didn't have a particular use in mind. When the owner of a local historic mansion gave me the beautiful columns——click! ——it was time to take the wood out of storage and put it to a good use.

—SIMON WHITELEY

CUTTING LIST

Code	Description	Qty	Material**	Dimensions**
A	Sides	2	2 x 8	2" x 8" x 12' (50.8 x 203.2 mm x 3.65 m)
B	Crossbeams	3	2 x 8	2" x 8" x 11' 8" (50.8 x 203.2 mm x 3.56 m)
C	Long rafters	8	2 x 8	2" x 8" x 8' (50.8 x 203.2 mm x 2.43 m)
D	Rafter Tails	8	2 x 8	2" x 8" x 2$^1/_2$' (50.8 x 203.2 mm x .76 m)
E	Triangle Braces	6	2 x 8	10" (254 mm) on each of 3 sides
F	Hollow Columns	6		8' to 10' tall (2.43 to 3 m)
G	Side Extensions	2	2 x 8	2" x 8" x 8' (50.8 x 203.2 mm x 2.43 m)

** Simon's material was rough-cut 2 x 8s, so the final measurement was indeed 2" x 8" (50.8 x 203.2 mm). Ordinary milled wood actually measures 1$^3/_4$" x 7$^1/_2$" (44.4 x 190.5 mm). Adjust all project measurements for the accurate dimensions of your materials.

ABOUT THE PERGOLA

We set up Simon's pergola in such a way that you could see all its parts to understand its construction principles. In reality, you'd need to make it more stable, so be sure to read the steps on securing the pergola below before you start.

The pergola is basically a square set on four columns (F), with the two sides (A), three crossbeams (B), and four long rafters (C) making the open roof above the square. Simon added another two columns (F) and the side extensions (G) to elongate the sides of the pergola on the back, which makes the pergola appear much bigger than it is.

MATERIALS
FOR THE PERGOLA

26 lock washers

26 flat washers

26 5-inch (127 mm) lag bolts

1 lb. #8 4-inch (101.6 mm) deck screws

1 lb. 8d galvanized finish nails

Semi-transparent white stain

MATERIALS
INSTALLATION

Steel plate, 16-inches (406 mm) square

$^1/_2$-inch (12.7 mm) rebar spikes, 3 feet (.6 m) long, 4 for each column

$^1/_2$-inch (12.7 mm) lag bolts, 8 inches (203 mm) long

TOOLS

Pair of sawhorses

Pencil

Nail set

Drill and drill bits: 1-inch (25.4 mm) spade bit and $^1/_4$-inch (6 mm) drill bit

Assortment of saws as needed: circular saw, jigsaw, and coping saw

Screw gun/drill combo with socket attachment

Paint roller

Paintbrush or rag

Sander or sandpaper

Wooden stakes, string, level, tape measure, to mark the pergola lay-out

Sledgehammer

Ladder, 8 to 10 feet (2.4 to 3 m)

Location: Level area large enough to assemble the pergola and erect it.

Helper Needed

You'll need a helper while erecting the pergola, and perhaps lifting and carrying lumber throughout the construction.

INSTRUCTIONS:
PERGOLA ROOF

1 Work on sawhorses in an adjacent area, using the photographs and figure 1 to guide you. Measure, then use the nail set to mark three sets of three holes on each of the sides (A) at their two ends and centers. In two steps, pre-drill all the holes. First, using the 1-inch (2.54 mm) spade bit, drill the holes 3/4 inch (19.05 mm) deep. (This will allow the lag bolt heads to countersink into the wood so they won't stick out.) Then drill in the center all the way through with the 1/4-inch (6 mm) drill bit to make holes for the lag screws.

2 Measure and mark the ends of the three crossbeams (B), pre-drilling three 1/4-inch (6 mm) holes the same way as in step 1.

3 After all holes have been pre-drilled, lay the two sides (A) and the three crossbeams (B) on the ground in the arrangement they will go together. Place lock washers and then the flat washers onto the lag bolts. Screw all 18 bolts into the pre-drilled holes.

4 Cut out the eight pieces that make up the four long rafters (C). (These will be connected in the middle later in step 8 so they will appear to be solid pieces.)

5 Enlarge the Rafter Tail Template to size and trace it onto one end of each of the four long rafters (C). At the other end of each rafter (C), mark a notch that is 1 x 4 inches (25.4 x 102 mm). (See the photo for guidance.) Cut both ends with the jigsaw and fine-tune your cuts with the coping saw. (You'll add the other notches in the centers of the long rafters later.)

6 Trace the rafter tail template onto each of the eight rafter tails (D). Cut them with the jigsaw and set them aside.

7 Measure the three crossbeams (B) and mark them so that the four pieces of the long rafters (C) will be placed properly. Use the diagram to guide you.

8 Take one of the long rafters (C) and place its notched end on the first mark on the crossbeam (B) in the center. Mark another notch, 2 x 4 inches (50.8 x 102 mm) deep, on the same long rafter (C) at the point where it will cross the side (A); cut out the notch with the jigsaw. Place the same long rafter (C) across the side (A) to make sure the notches have been cut properly and the rafter lines up securely. If it does, trace this notch onto the remaining three scrolled ends of the long rafters (C) and cut them out. You now have four rafter pieces with two notches each.

9 Place all four long rafters (C) on top of the crossbeams (B) and sides (A). Mark on each long rafter (C) where you'll place the lag bolts above the notch on their scrolled ends. (See diagram.) Repeating the same sequence as the procedure from step 3, screw in the lag bolts, lock washers, and regular washers. Then use the screw gun and the 4-inch (102 mm) decking screws to toenail (screw in from the side on an angle) each notched end at the center. (See diagram.) You've now completed the square top.

10 Number each piece, then carefully disassemble them.

11 Paint each piece with the roller and semi-transparent stain. Use

the brush for details. Let everything set for about five minutes, then wipe it off with a rag, removing some of the stain but leaving heavy traces of white color. This makes the pieces blend with the old columns better. Let everything dry.

INSTRUCTIONS:
INSTALLATION

12 See figure 2. Place a column carefully on two sawhorses so you can work safely. Measure then pre-drill ³/₄-inch (19.05 mm) holes in the center of the plate to match the rim of the column. See figure 2 to guide you. Then pre-drill the holes for the rebar. Drive the bolts through the plate into the column.

13 Use the stakes, string, tape measure, and level to mark the location of each of the four columns.

14 With your helper, turn the column right side up and position it. With the sledgehammer, bend over each spike at the top so it doesn't go through the hole. (See figure 2.) Drive the rebar spikes into the ground.

15 Repeat steps 12 through 14 for each column.

16 Re-check each column for squareness by placing a length of string diagonally between columns at opposite corners. Both distances should measure the same.

17 When you are confident that the columns are placed correctly, using the ladder, place the sides (A) across two of the columns (F), then place the two outer crossbeams (B). Attach the pieces using the same lag bolt-washer process from step 3. Repeat for the remaining side (A) and the other outer crossbeam (B). See the diagram.

18 Adjust the square of the boards if needed, then screw in the remaining screws to secure them. Place the center crossbeam (B) and screw it in, too.

19 Place the triangle braces (E) on top of the column capitals and into the 45° angles between the sides (A) and outer crossbeams (B). From above the braces, toenail them into the top of the column capitals.

20 One at a time, in order as you numbered them in step 10, place the long rafters (C). Re-attach them to the crossbeams (B) in the holes you previously drilled in step 8.

21 Toenail in the rafter tails (D) to the ends of the sides (A) and the crossbeams (B).

22 Optional: If you wish to extend the back sides with two columns (F) and the side extenders (G), do that now. Follow the instructions in steps 12 through 14.

23 Relax, admire your work, then have your party!

24 After you've recovered from admiring your work and having your party, disassemble everything to set up in the next party location.

ABOUT PERMANENT
INSTALLATION

If you wish to make a permanent installation, see page 25 for basic information on digging postholes. Pergolas, like arbors, should be a minimum of 7 feet (2.1 m) tall to provide adequate headroom. One-third of the aboveground height of a column should be underground. This means if you wanted columns at the minimum height of 7 feet (2.1 m) aboveground, the columns before insertion would have to measure at least 9' 4" (2.84 m) tall.

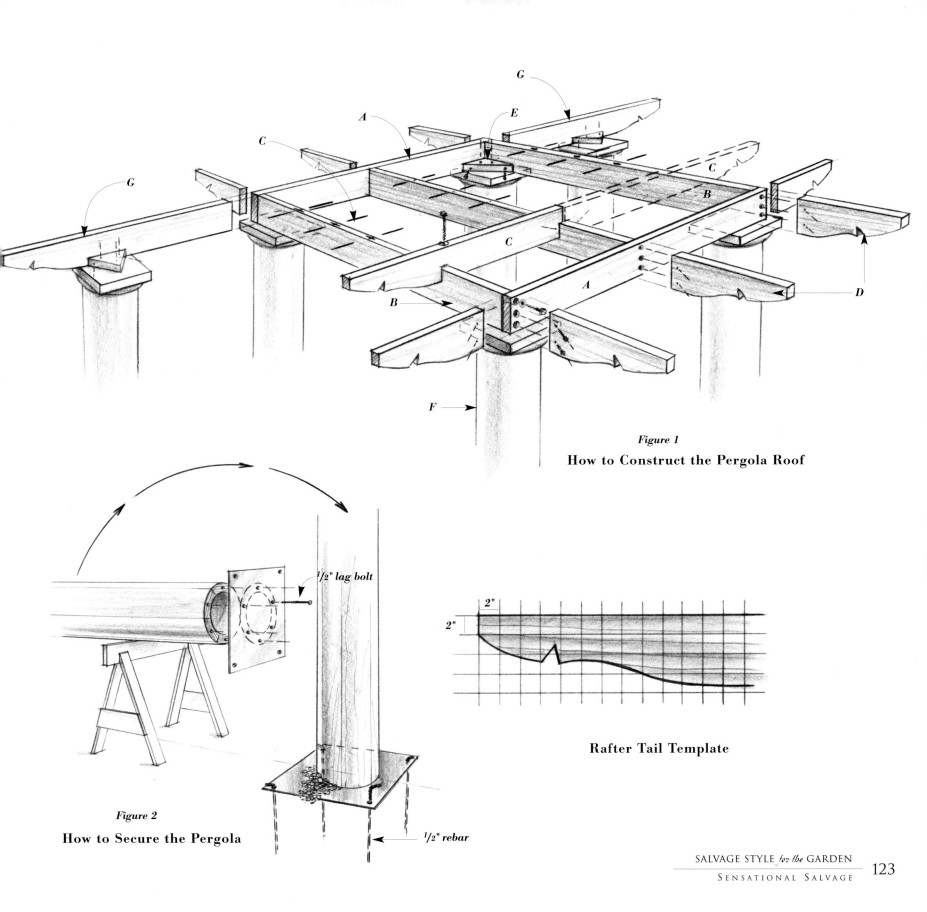

A

C

G

G

E

C

B

G

B

C

A

D

B

F

Figure 1

How to Construct the Pergola Roof

$^1/_2$" lag bolt

Figure 2

How to Secure the Pergola

$^1/_2$" rebar

2"

2"

Rafter Tail Template

VINTAGE GLASS WINDOW

THIS SALVAGE-STYLE ART WINDOW MAKES STUNNING USE OF VINTAGE WAVY GLASS—ONE OF THOSE WONDERFUL SALVAGE MATERIALS THAT IS READILY AVAILABLE BUT OFTEN OVERLOOKED. FIRST TRY YOUR HAND AT THE SIMPLE DESIGN SHOWN HERE, THEN TACKLE COMBINING CLEAR AND COLORED GLASS IN MORE ELABORATE DESIGNS.

It's easy to find old wavy glass, particularly in big single panes. People want windows with multiple frames so they pass by the single-frame windows, leaving a ton of wavy glass available to people who want to use it creatively."

– CHRISTI WHITELEY

MATERIALS

Old wooden window frame with single pane of wavy glass

A square piece of colored glass, salvaged or new

Lead solder for glass, if you are doing all the work yourself

Paste wax

Glaziers points

Glaziers putty (optional)

Hooks for hanging

TOOLS

5-in-1 painter's tool or scraper

Glass cutter

Marker

Sander or sandpaper used with water

Paintbrush (optional)

INSTRUCTIONS

1 Select a flat surface on which you can work safely with the glass. With the painter's tool or scraper, remove the old glazing and glaziers points from the window. Carefully remove the clear wavy glass. (If you don't have one solid piece of glass, you can use enough pieces of broken glass to create a window-sized pane.)

2 Mark the glass into four equal parts, connecting at the center. With the glass cutter, cut out the four pieces.

3 Lay the four pieces on your working surface and place the colored decorative piece of glass in the center. With the marker, trace the shape of the decorative piece onto the clear pieces. (See the project photos to guide you.) Cut the clear glass pieces along the marked lines. You now have five pieces.

4 If you know how to re-attach the pieces with lead solder, do it now. If not, take them to a trained stained glass worker to have them soldered into one piece.

5 If necessary, using water, sand any excess old paint off the wooden window frame and then coat it with the paste wax. The wax makes rainwater run off the window and gives it a nice weathered, but finished, look.

6 Put the newly leaded glass piece back into the frame and secure with new glaziers points. You don't need to reglaze the window if you're using it as a decorative piece. But if you plan to use it as a functional window, reglaze it.

7 Add hooks to the top of the window and hang it any place where the sun will strike it.

LOOK CLOSELY AT WAVY GLASS

Determine which kind of glass you have. The glassmaking process left telltale signs on the glass, which you can see if you look at it from the side. Crown glass was made for centuries, until about the 1850s. It has distinctive spirals or curved ripples on it. If you do indeed have crown glass, unless it's already broken into pieces, you probably don't want to cut it.

Cylinder glass was made after crown glass, until the end of the twentieth century. Its manufacturing process left faint parallel ripples on it. Also, cylinder glass has a smooth side and a rough side. Cut cylinder glass from the smooth side so it's easier to make a clean cut.

SPARKLING PARTY MOBILE

No matter where you hang it, you'll be celebrating salvage style every day with this sparkling mobile. After you've gathered all the parts, you can put the mobile together in a few hours—just in time to show it off at the party!

I never worry if I plan one thing and something else turns up. This project started off as a windchime and then, with all the chandelier pieces I'd found in a box lot at an auction, it ended up being a mobile.

— CHRISTI WHITELEY

MATERIALS

Dangles:

9 spindles, of different sizes

17 wooden curtain rings

Lots of chandelier drop crystals

Lots of crystal chains

2 chair rungs

Length of vintage chain

Lots of screw eyes

4 cup hooks

TOOLS

Tape measure

Permanent marker

INSTRUCTIONS

1 The trick to making the mobile is to create balance among all the elements. Lay each dangle flat on the table and plan its composition before you start to hang it. Include the spindles, the curtain rings, and the chandelier drop crystals, connecting them with screw eyes as needed.

2 Use the photos to guide you to measure and mark the two rungs that will be the horizontal pieces from which the dangles hang.

■ Mark on the center of both the top and bottom lengths and screw in screw eyes.

■ Mark along the bottom lengths of both rungs, evenly spaced from the center. After you've determined at which marks you want to hang the dangles, screw in screw eyes for them.

3 Attach the chain to the top center screw eye on the top rung, then attach that by its center bottom screw eye to the top center of the lower rung. Hang up these top pieces and work on the mobile while it's in this position.

4 Screw a screw eye into the top of one of the weighty spindles. Hang the spindle from the center of the lower rung.

5 Working in pairs now to keep things in balance, hang a dangle at both sides of the top rung. Then continue to hang the other dangles until you hang them all and they are in balance. Lengthen the dangles with more pieces, as you wish.

6 Add cup hooks to the ends of both rungs. Hang large crystals and drape lots of crystal chains across the mobile to connect the four ends.

Sensational SALVAGE

In the center of a new fountain, a lovely old concrete medallion adds a touch of timelessness. DESIGN BY PEEPLES-KIMAK DESIGN ASSOCIATES

This gazebo is made entirely from salvage materials. The stunning cupola was actually found discarded by the side of the road! DESIGN BY PEEPLES-KIMAK DESIGN ASSOCIATES

This spectacular bench is a simple combination of an iron gate, a salvaged bed frame, and bricks that once paved a city sidewalk. DESIGN BY JOHNNY LEE AND KATINA JONES

This stunning fountain is made from giant-sized vestiges of our rural past: a millstone and a syrup kettle.
PHOTO BY HENRY HINE, COURTESY OF ANNE HATHAWAY MILLSTONES

Salvaged metal parts are welded to new steel rebar to create this pretty patio table.
DESIGN BY DANA MARGARET IRWIN
FABRICATED BY LARRY FREER

Years of design and welding experience went into this handsome arbor made from antique fencing.
DESIGN BY BRAD OLIVER

Made from salvaged windows and doors, this greenhouse protects growing plants all year long.
DESIGN AND PHOTO BY G. MICHAEL SHOUP, ANTIQUE ROSE EMPORIUM

Early Victorian gates look perfectly at home in a modern setting.
COURTESY OF UNIQUITIES ARCHITECTURAL ANTIQUES

The main structure of this sunroom is new pressure-treated wood. The embellishments, however, are vintage architectural details found in local fleamarkets. Notice the transformation of salvaged items such as doors, porch railings, balusters, garden edging, and hardware.

In this little girl's dream playhouse, the door, arch, window box, and shutter-slat cupola are made from architectural salvage.

DESIGNS AND PHOTOS BY DAVID WILGUS

Worn and discarded pieces of the past… orphaned fragments of other people's lives… as our ever-changing society replaces old with new, I find magic by resurrecting small parts of the past and making them new.

—SIMONE WILSON

FANCY FLYING SPINDLES

An old chair leg, a piece of a banister railing, part of baby's crib—turn a spindle with any previous life into a wonderful specimen of salvage style. Old spindles often come with years of "fresh" coats of paint, so sometimes you don't even have to paint them to set them off on their flights of fancy.

MATERIALS

1 Spindle

Salvaged sheet metal, about 2 square feet (.6 m), such as from old barn roofing

3 or 4 ³/4-inch (1.9 cm) screws

Baling wire

Marker

Paint and varnish (optional)

TOOLS

Paintbrush (optional)

Drill

Screwdriver

Plasma cutter or tin snips

Hammer

Nail set

INSTRUCTIONS

1 If you wish, paint the spindle, letting its shapes inspire vibrant color combinations. If your bug will spend its days outdoors, coat its body with a heavy outdoor varnish and let it dry completely.

2 Make the antennae. Your spindle should have a top and a bottom, meaning the head of the bug on one end, and its tail on the other. Predrill a hole in the middle of the top of the spindle and drive a screw halfway into the hole. At its halfway point, wrap a very long piece of the wire around the screw. Tighten the screw so that wire is secured firmly to the top of the bug. Curl the opposite ends of the wire into fantastical antennae shapes.

3 If you're making a dragonfly, you may want to also add a tail by wrapping baling wire around the end of the spindle.

4 Make the wings. The size of your bug body will determine the size of its wings. Draw the shape of wings on the sheet metal and cut out the shape with the plasma cutter or tin snips. The plasma cutter will certainly make the job easier, but the tin snips will work adequately. Use the hammer and nail set to punch two holes (vertically, one on top of the other) in the middle of the set of wings. (If you have a plasma cutter, use it to cut out

patterns in the wings if you wish.)

5 Position the bug body face down and place the wings on its back. Pre-drill and screw on the wings through the holes you punched in them in the previous step.

6 Make the hookhanger. Cut a length of wire that is suitable for the size of the hook, usually a little less than 12 inches (30.5 cm). Mark a spot about halfway up the length of the body and drive a screw in partway. Wrap one end of the wire around the bottom screw in the wing and the other in the screw you just placed. Tighten them both. Test the balance of the hook, shaping and bending the hanging wire to find the right spot on it from which to hang the bug.

LAWN CHESS SET

ESIGNER JEFF HAMILTON HAD WANTED TO MAKE A LAWN CHESS SET FOR YEARS, BUT FELT DAUNTED BY WHAT SEEMED AN OVERWHELMING AND EXPENSIVE PROJECT. (AFTER ALL, THERE ARE 32 PIECES IN A CHESS SET!) THE INSPIRATION TO FIND AND USE SALVAGED PIECES SIMPLIFIED THE PROCESS AND MADE IT AFFORDABLE. ALL HE HAD LEFT TO FIND WAS A FEW FREE WEEKENDS.

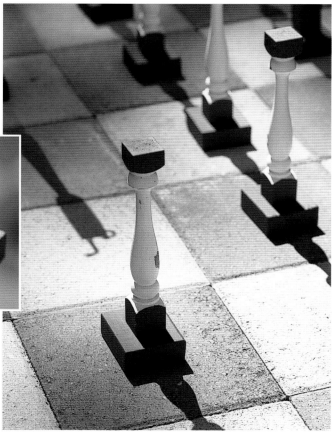

I've always loved taking different things, especially old salvaged objects, and putting them together to make something new. The garden chess set is the ultimate use of turning old things not only into art, but into a functional game you can play.

— JEFF HAMILTON

MATERIALS:

THE CHESS PIECES

16 short spindles for the pawns

16 tall spindles for the tall pieces

Wooden blocks

32 wooden "bottom" blocks for all the pieces, cut from old 2 x 4s each 2 inches (5 cm) tall

6 wooden "top" blocks for bishops and the kings, 2 inches square x 1 inch tall (5 cm sq x 2.5 cm)

4 wooden "queen-top" blocks for the queens, 1-1/2 inches square x 3 inches tall (3.8 cm sq. x 7.6 cm)

2 wooden "king-topmost" blocks, same as the "queen-tops" above

Paint, 1 pint (.47 L) each of two contrasting colors of your choice

Wood glue

All purpose glue/cement glue

MATERIALS:

THE DECORATIVE TOPS OF THE PIECES

16 small hinges for the rooks

4 large coat hooks for the knights

4 teardrop-shaped curtain rod finials for the bishops

2 small crystal doorknobs for the queens

2 large crystal doorknobs for the kings

Small wooden dowels, 1 inch (2.5 cm) long, as needed

MATERIALS:

THE CHESS BOARD

32 gray landscape pavers 12 x 12 inches (.3 m x .3 m)

32 red landscape pavers 12 x 12 inches (.3 m x .3 m)

4 landscape timbers, 8 feet (2.4 m) long

TOOLS:

THE CHESS PIECES

Hammer

Nails

Circular saw

Drill

Phillips head screwdriver

Tape measure

T square

TOOLS:

THE CHESS BOARD

Level

Shovel

All-purpose sand as needed

Wheelbarrow

Rubber mallet

BEFORE YOU START

Make sure you actually have enough flat space in your garden to accommodate the chess game. The board itself is 8 feet (2.4 m) square, and you'll want another 4 feet (1.2 m) on both sides for room to play, so you'll need a space that is at least 12 feet (3.6 m) square.

INSTRUCTIONS:

THE PIECES

1 Attach wooden blocks to all the spindles to make them stable and create different heights.

■ Drill a $^1/_8$-inch (3 mm) hole in the center of the 32 bottom blocks and screw each one into the bottom of a spindle.

■ With the wood glue, attach one "top" block to the center tops of six of the tall spindles. These are for the four bishops and the lower tier of the two kings. Wait until the blocks on the kings dry completely, then glue the topmost blocks onto each one.

- With the wood glue, attach one "queen top" block to the top of each of two tall spindles.

- Don't put blocks on the remaining eight tall spindles. These will become the rooks and the knights in step 3.

2 Divide the pieces into two complete sets and paint each set with a different color of your choice. Paint just the top and bottom sections and leave the middle in its original salvaged look. Jeff chose red-orange and purple because they contrasted nicely and worked with his landscaping colors.

3 Attach the salvaged hardware decorative tops to the tall pieces. Use any kind of salvage you want, but make sure all the similar pieces, such as the rooks, etc. look similar. If you like the sparkle of the old hardware and crystal pieces, do what Jeff did:

- *Decorate the rooks:* Place one of the hinges at the top corner of a tall spindle without a top block. Mark the location of the hinge holes, drill pilot holes, and attach hinge with screws. Repeat for each of the other three corners for the first spindle. Repeat the whole process for the other three rooks

- *Decorate the knights:* Mark the top center of the spindle top, drill pilot

holes, and then screw in the coat hooks.

- *Decorate the bishops:* Mark the tops of the four spindles with top blocks, drill pilot poles, then securely screw in the curtain rod finials.

- *Decorate the queens:* Drill a 1/4-inch (6mm) hole in the top of each queen block of wood. If your doorknob comes with the rod attached to it, just apply glue to it and insert it into the hole. If the rod is missing, you can make rods out of the wooden dowels. Measure the doorknob pin and get a dowel with the same diameter. Apply wood glue to the dowel and insert it into the hole in the wood. Apply glue to the cavity in the doorknob and slip it securely over the top of the dowel.

- *Decorate the kings:* Follow the same instructions as for decorating the queens, using the larger crystal doorknobs.

INSTRUCTIONS: THE CHESS BOARD

1 Clear off the space in your yard by removing grass, leaves, rocks, and mulch from the surface until you reach the clay surface underneath the topsoil. Of course, if you've already got a flat gravel or concrete surface, go ahead and use it.

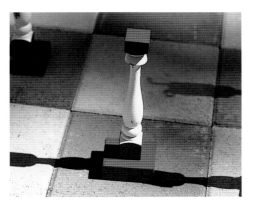

2 Use the level and one of the 8-foot (2.4 m) landscape timbers to check if your space is truly level. If it needs leveling, add sand or gravel as needed and keep checking with the level.

3 Start at one corner of the location where the board will be laid. Pour the sand into your wheelbarrow and spread a shovelful or two onto the clay. In the lower right corner of one of the sides that will face a player, place a gray paver on the sand. (On a chess board, the lower right corner square of the two sides that face the players is always the lighter color.)

4 Lightly tamp the paver with the rubber mallet to level it, and then check with the level and the 2 x 4. Repeat with each of the next seven pavers in the first row, alternating the colors of the pavers as you go along. Repeat for the remaining seven rows, for a total of eight rows with eight pavers each.

HAPPY GARDEN BIRD

WOODEN BIRDS FOUND MANY YEARS AGO IN THE CLOSET OF AN OLD HOUSE INSPIRED SIMON WHITELEY TO PUT HIS OWN SPIN ON THE DESIGN. MADE OF VINTAGE MATERIALS BUT BRIGHTLY COLORED WITH NEW PAINT, THE BIRD SEEMS TO FLY HAPPILY BACK AND FORTH BETWEEN OLD AND NEW.

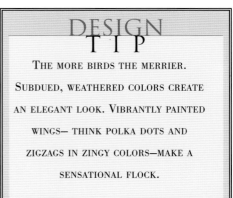

DESIGN TIP

THE MORE BIRDS THE MERRIER. SUBDUED, WEATHERED COLORS CREATE AN ELEGANT LOOK. VIBRANTLY PAINTED WINGS— THINK POLKA DOTS AND ZIGZAGS IN ZINGY COLORS—MAKE A SENSATIONAL FLOCK.

MATERIALS

1 sheet of malleable metal, such as tin, aluminum, or copper

1 piece of 3/4-inch (1.9 cm) scrap wood, big enough for the bird pattern

Paint or stain

Felt-tip black marker

Small nails

Threaded screw eyes, medium size

Length of old chain, such as a rusty plumber's chain

1 S-hook

TOOLS

Jigsaw

Sander or sandpaper

Power drill and bits (optional)

Tin snips

File

Round-headed hammer

Punch or sturdy nail

INSTRUCTIONS

1 Draw the pattern of a bird on the scrap of wood, or use the template below. With the jigsaw, cut out the pattern. Sand the hard edges. Paint or stain the wood. To give it texture, let it sit a bit after you paint it, then wipe it down and let it dry completely.

2 Use the drill to make eyes on both sides of the bird's head. Drill just enough to make half-circle impressions, then color them with the black marker. Or, if you wish, just draw on the eyes with the marker.

3 Draw your own wings on the metal, or use the template. The wings should be a symmetrical pattern so the bird will balance properly. Use the tin snips to cut out the wings. File smooth any sharp edges.

4 With your hands (or the hammer), bend and shape the curves of the wings to fit the arch of the back of the bird. Use the punch or a nail to make holes in the wings where you want to attach them to the bird's body. Then attach the wings with screws through the pre-punched holes.

5 Screw the screw eye into the arch of the bird's back at a place that nicely 'balances' the bird when it's suspended.

6 Attach the desired length of chain to the screw eye. Hang an S-hook at the end of the chain and hang the bird.

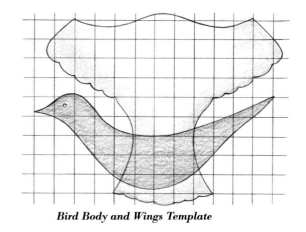

Bird Body and Wings Template

GAZING BALL SCARECROW

THERE'S NO SUCH THING AS AN ORDINARY CORN PATCH IF IT'S GUARDED BY A SALVAGE STYLE SCARECROW. IMAGINE A WHOLE FAMILY OF SCARECROWS, MADE FROM ALL KINDS OF SALVAGED POSTS AND CORBELS, EACH WITH A DIFFERENT HEAD BLAZING IN THE SUN.

INSTRUCTIONS

1 Lay the porch post and corbels on the ground.

2 Using the tape measure, measure and mark 3 inches (7.6 cm) down from the top of the post on two opposite sides. Using the nail gun, attach the corbels evenly to the post below the marks. (If you don't have a nail gun, pre-drill holes before you drive the nails. Old wood is so dense that if you don't take such precautions, you could split it.)

3 With the screw gun and the 1-inch (5 cm) screws, attach each L-bracket to the post and the corbel at the 45° angle where they meet.

4 Place the scarecrow in the garden. See page 25 for information on posthole digging. Or, sink into wet concrete an iron post with 3 feet (.9 m) extending above ground, and slip the hollow post over it.

5 After the post is stabilized, place the neck of the gazing ball into the top of the porch post.

If you want your scarecrow to wear a traditional hat and scarf, just add a few more steps.

1 Screw in a screw eye about 1 inch (2.5 cm) above each corbel.

2 Thread strands of rope through the screw eyes and the strap on the hat; pull tight and knot. This will hold the hat and add a little extra security to the gazing ball. Tie an old scarf around the bottom of the gazing ball to add some color.

MATERIALS

Square porch post with hollow center, about 6 feet (1.8 m) in height, for the body

2 large corbels for the arms

Gazing ball (new or old) for the head

2 2-inch (5 cm) L-brackets

Optional: screw eyes, rope, old hat, scarf

TOOLS

Tape measure

hammer or nail gun and 3-inch (7.6 cm) finish nails

Power drill/screw gun if you predrill before you nail

1-inch (2.5 cm) wood screws

"You have to make a scarecrow!" my friend insisted. Simon and I had this odd square hollow porch post that no one wanted. We thought it would make a great scarecrow body. And the neck of the gazing ball head slipped right into it.

– CHRISTI WHITELEY

GIANT TIN PINWHEEL

INSPIRED BY THE BEAUTY OF TIN CEILING TILES HE'D SALVAGED FROM A CENTURY-OLD BUILDING, JEFF BURGNER DESIGNED HIS GIANT PINWHEEL TO SHOW OFF BOTH SIDES OF THE TIN AT THE SAME TIME.

INSTRUCTIONS

1 With the tin snips, cut two pieces of tin into squares and mark their centers. To find the center, use the straightedge and the pencil, and draw diagonal, vertical, and horizontal lines—the point at which all the lines intersect is the center.

2 Make your own pinwheel design. Or enlarge the template (on page 146) on a photocopier to match the size you want. (The pinwheel in the photo used pieces of tin that were 3 x 3 feet [.9 m]). If you want a very sturdy template, just tape the copier paper onto a piece of cardboard and cut out the shape from that.

3 With the marker, trace the shape of the template onto the sheets of tin. Use the tin snips to cut four leaves of the pinwheel, one at each corner. Repeat on the second sheet of tin.

4 Lay the two sheets of tin, rust side up, on top of one another, aligning the top piece at about a 20° angle to the bottom piece. Turn them so the cuts in the tin interlock the two pieces. Fold every other leaf into the center. Bend the other leaves at their edges so they'll catch the wind.

5 Bend the all the leaves to join in the center, making the pinwheel. Drill holes in the tips of the leaves in four spots at the center point. Fasten the leaves together with the bolts and matching nuts.

MATERIALS

Sheets of tin ceiling, cut to your desired length. The ones in the photo were 3 feet (.9m) wide.

Wooden post that is tall and sturdy enough to hold the pinwheel

4 nuts and 4 bolts to secure the leaves of the pinwheel to the center

1 bolt, at least 4 inches (10.2 cm) long, and 2 matching nuts to secure the pinwheel to the post

TOOLS

Tin snips

Marker

Straightedge

Pencil

Power drill and bits

Sledgehammer

6 Cut the post to your desired length and drill a hole into it where you will place the center of the pinwheel.

7 Drill a hole into the center of the pinwheel. Insert the long bolt and a matching nut through the hole and secure it on the other side with another nut. (Make sure that the bolt is long enough to allow the pinwheel

to clear the post.) Be sure the nuts aren't fastened too tightly or the pinwheel won't spin.

8 Hammer the post into the ground. Give the pinwheel a first hearty spin, then let the wind take over. (If you've made your pinwheel really big, then see page 25 for instructions on digging post-holes so you can secure it permanently.)

9 Keep the pinwheel well-oiled so it will spin freely all year long.

DESIGN TIP

IF YOU WANT A BRIGHTLY COLORED BUT WEATHERED-LOOKING PINWHEEL, SEE PAINTING TIPS ON PAGE 19.

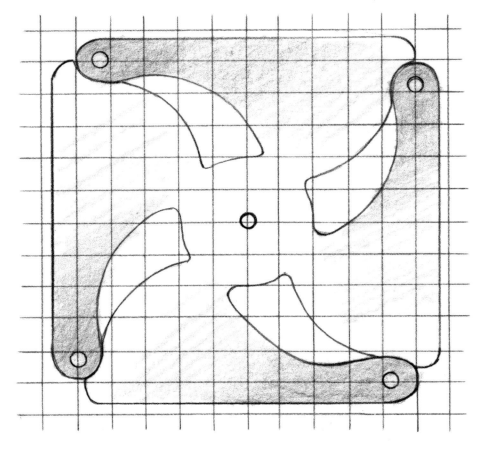

Pinwheel Template

SALVAGE TREASURES WINDOW

"BUTTERFLIES IN SEARCH OF NECTAR THROUGH FUN HOUSE OF MIRRORS" IS WHAT DESIGNER DIANA LIGHT CALLS HER FANTASTIC SALVAGE TREASURES WINDOW. SHE MADE IT FROM AN OLD WINDOW FRAME, RUSTY HINGES AND CHAINS, SALVAGED GLASS AND MIRRORS, ALUMINUM SHEETS, CHANDELIER CRYSTALS, DOORKNOB ROSETTES—OH, AND LET'S NOT FORGET THE TOOTHBRUSH HOLDER SHE SAVED FROM HER OLD BATHROOM!

Ooooo, just have fun!

— DIANA LIGHT

SALVAGE MATERIALS

Old wooden window frame, with or without glass

Salvaged glass and mirror pieces

Rusty hinges with one or two ball ends, large and small sizes

Aluminum sheets, thin, so they can be cut with tin snips

Rusty baling wire

Rusty chains, small and large, such as from toilet tanks or old windows

Chandelier crystals

Toothbrush holder

Rosettes from doorknobs

4 Drawer pull escutcheons

OTHER MATERIALS

Newspapers (optional)

Protective gloves and glasses

Pencil

All-purpose cleaner and water

Lubricating oil

Rubbing alcohol (optional)

Dishwasher-safe transparent and/or translucent glass paints

Nails, both new and rusty

8 lb. fishing line

Tape

Glues: white craft or wood glue, and clear waterproof adhesive for glass

TOOLS

Putty knife

Hammer

Palm sander

Ruler or other straightedge

Marker

Glass cutter

Tin snips

Small Hammer

Paintbrushes as needed

Grommet setter (optional)

Pliers

Wire cutters

Power drill with drill bits

INSTRUCTIONS

1 With water and the putty knife, chip away any loose wood and paint from the window frame. (See the precautions on lead-based paint on page 19.) If there is glass in the window, try to take out the whole pane by first removing the glaziers putty. If you can't, then lay newspaper under and over the glass and hit it with the hammer. Wearing protective gloves and glasses, carefully pull out the glass. Keep the larger pieces and safely discard the rest. Let the wood dry.

2 If you want, sand through the top layers of paint to find out what's hidden underneath as Diana did to discover lovely layers of old pale purple and green paint.

3 Clean the glass and mirrors well so paint or dirt doesn't dull your cutter. With the ruler (or straightedge) and the permanent marker, measure and mark squares of glass and mirror, such as $1\frac{1}{2}$-inch (3.8 cm) to 2-inch (5 cm) squares of glass and 1-inch (2.5 cm) squares of mirror. Hold the glass cutter upright with one hand and grasp the end of the handle with the other, putting pressure on it to steady the cut on the glass and pull it smoothly and evenly. Cut enough squares to glue them back-to-back on the fishing line in step 11.

4 Make the butterflies. Spray the lubricating oil on the rusty hinges until you can pry them open (with tools such as a small hammer) and get them moving. (Notice in the project photo that some butterflies have more open wings than others, that's fine.) Lay the hinges flat on the aluminum and pencil-draw two-wing shapes that suit the hinges.

5 Cut out the wings with the tin snips. Make two holes in the wings to line up with holes in the flat sides of the hinge—use a grommet setter to make nice round holes, or just use a hammer and nail. Punch decorative holes on the wing edges.

6 Here's how to secure a hinge to a pair of wings. With the pliers, form rusty baling wire into the shape of a long staple—two long sides and a shorter flat top that is the same length as the distance between the two holes in the wing. Then slip the long ends through the holes in the wing and the side of the hinge (the wire will lie nice and flat since you shaped the flat top already) and secure it to itself on the inside of the wings. Wrap another piece of wire around the ball end of the hinge and shape it into two antennae.

7 To make the flower, use the tin snips to cut out petal shapes from the aluminum. Use the nail and hammer to punch holes into the center of the flower and then thread rusty wires into them to make the stamen. Curl the wires on the back of the flower to keep them from pulling all the way out.

8 Clean the glass pieces—rubbing alcohol can help take off the permanent marker lines. Follow the manufacturer's instructions on the paint bottles and color the pieces. Bake them, if needed. Make your own colors, or do what Diana did and brush on an iridescent medium mixed with the purple and green colors she chose to match the old paint on the wood

frame. Try a crackling medium for different results.

9 Lay the window flat and arrange all the objects where you want them: butterflies, squares of glass and mirror, and the chandelier crystals.

10 Measure and mark on the back of each window frame section where you want your fishing lines to hang. Cut the fishing lines the height of the sections, leaving an extra 6 inches (15.2 cm) on each end for tying. Drive in small nails at the marks on both the top and bottom of each section.

11 Tape each piece of line onto your work surface. Glue the glass pieces back-to-back so they sandwich the fishing line between them

and let them dry. Do the same with mirror pieces. Tie the lines to the nails on the top of the muntins, pull taut, and attach on the bottom nails too.

12 With the drill, pre-drill holes in the sections of the window where you want to hang the butterflies. Squeeze a little glue in the hole, then drive in the nail, but leave about 1/2 inch (1.3 cm) exposed. Use the pliers and wire cutters to affix the chains to the butterflies and then to the nails. Use fishing line to tie crystals to the butterflies if you wish.

13 Make the windchime in the top center pane. Screw the toothbrush holder into the top of the pane. With the hammer and nail make a hole in each rosette disc. With the pliers and wire cutters, attach chains from the toothbrush holder to each rosette, hanging them at different lengths so they'll ring together when the wind blows.

14 Pre-drill a hole on the frame and then hammer the flower into it.

15 Screw the drawer pull escutcheons to the top two corners on both the front and back sides of the window frame. Use big chain looped through the drawer pull handles to hang the window.

FANTASTIC FLAMINGOS & FRIENDS

GARDEN FLAMINGOS WILL NEVER BE THE SAME AFTER THIS FANTASTIC SALVAGE METAL BIRD MOVES INTO THE NEIGHBORHOOD! WITH DESIGNER JIMMY HOPKINS' GUIDANCE AND SOME BASIC WELDING KNOWLEDGE AND TOOLS, YOU CAN MAKE A WHOLE MENAGERIE OF YARD ANIMALS. IF YOU DON'T WELD, THEN CONCENTRATE ON COLLECTING THE SALVAGED METAL PARTS AND DESIGNING HOW TO COMBINE THEM—AND THEN FIND SOMEONE WITH EXPERTISE TO WELD THEM TOGETHER FOR YOU.

Growing up on a farm with my granddaddy, I learned to love animals, so it was just natural for me to make animal figures... A little metal bull is what got me started. I made this one piece and everybody loved it. They said, "Make some more!" So I did. I made more and made them bigger. I've probably made enough animals by now to fill a zoo!

—JIMMY HOPKINS

MATERIALS

1 regular round-nose shovel with the handle removed

8 feet (2.4 m) of ¹/₂-inch (1.3 cm) rebar

1¹/₂ feet (.4 m) of ⁵/₈-inch (1.6 cm) rebar for the neck

1 blade guard from a sickle bar mower

2 ⁵/₁₆-inch (8mm) hex nuts

Permanent marker

TOOLS

Oxy/acetylene torch

Chop saw or hacksaw

Bench vise

Electric arc welder

Tape measure or ruler

Pliers

Marker

Safety Alert: The welding process produces lots of red hot metal and sparks, meaning you must always think "Safety First". Remove all combustibles from the area. Observe all safety warnings on your tools. Wear adequate protection including welding gloves, goggles, and shield. Cover all exposed areas of your body.

INSTRUCTIONS

1 Use the torch to cut off the neck of the shovel. Don't discard the neck; save it for another project. Turn the shovel over and use the torch to split it down the middle. (The torch superheats the metal and then uses a high volume of clean oxygen to blow the molten metal from the area that you are trying to cut.) Set the two halves of the shovel aside to cool, or quench them under a stream of cool water. *Caution:* Cooling the metal with water will produce a short burst of steam, which can cause severe burns.

2 With the chop saw (or hacksaw or other metal cutting saw), cut the 8-foot (2.4m) length of ¹/₂-inch (1.3 cm) rebar into all the pieces you need for the legs. The flamingo in the photo used the following pieces:

2 pieces 30 inches (76.2 cm) long

1 piece 6 inches (15.2 cm) long

2 pieces 3¹/₂ inches (8.9 cm) long

Save the 22-inch (58.4 cm) piece of rebar that remains to fashion two internal braces to be used during assembly in step 11.

3 Here's how to create the classic folded flamingo leg: Measure and mark 6 inches (15.2 cm) from an end of one of the 30-inch (76.2 cm) pieces of rebar—this is where the first bend will be. Clamp the short end into the bench vise, and bend the piece at a slight angle (approximately 15°), as you heat it. Use the torch to heat the metal at the point of the bend. Heat the entire area of the angle, rather than concentrating on one point, to allow the metal to bend more easily and prevent it from stretching. Remove this piece from the vise and let it cool.

4 Measure 18 inches (45.7 cm) from the first bend to mark where the second bend will be. Clamp the leg in the vise up to the first bend, so that the rebar is at a right angle to the vise jaws. With the torch, heat the leg at the new mark, remembering to heat ¹/₂ to ³/₄ inch (1.3 to 1.9 cm) on both sides of the mark to get it hot evenly. You'll know it's ready to be bent when the metal in this area begins to turn cherry red.

5 At this point, bend the leg back toward the vise. Bend the metal until you achieve the desired angle, 30° to 45°. Remove from the vise and cool.

6 Now measure 2 or 3 inches (5 or 7.6 cm) from the end that has not been bent. Clamp this end in the vise, heat it with the torch and bend it up to a right angle. This completes the first leg.

7 To make the second leg, save the top 2 inches (5 cm) of the rebar to weld onto the body of the bird later

in step 9, and shape the leg as you like. Generally people prefer the second leg to be straight, as if the bird is standing on it, with his other leg tucked up.

8 Now make the S-shaped neck using the 5/8-inch (1.6 cm) diameter rebar. (You may want to draw the desired shape on large sheet of paper to guide you as you work.) Again you'll need the vise, the torch, and the length of pipe for leverage while bending. Because the metal that you're bending is thicker than the legs, it will require longer heating time and a little more leverage. Remember to work the metal slowly, heating as you make your bend, and letting the bend progress slowly. When you have finished, let it cool completely.

9 Now you're ready to assemble and weld the bird's body to the legs. Clamp the first leg, the bended one (from steps 3 to 6), into the vise. Take one of the shovel halves and position it so it hits the leg right at the first bend; weld it there. Let it cool and remove it from the vise. Repeat for the other shovel half and the other leg, letting both shovel-leg sections cool completely.

10 Clamp the first section back into the vise in the standing position. Hold the other section in place so the two shovel halves touch at the top front. Weld this seam together, holding until the weld joint cools and you've created the body.

When I told my father that I wanted to make welded sculptures that people would buy for their gardens, he shook his head and said "That'll happen when pigs fly." After I completely sold out my first batch of "critters," Dad bought me a trailer to haul them to the next show. And I made lots of "flying pigs" from that day on!

—JIMMY HOPKINS

11 Make sure that all of your welds suit you and the angles match up. (Remember, if you don't like the angles, you can re-weld until you do.) Now add two braces to the inside of the bird's body to strengthen it and help keep its shape. (Look closely at the photo and you'll see only one brace, but there should be two.) Measure the front opening of the body below where you just welded the shovel halves; transfer that measurement to the remaining rebar brace piece that you had left from the legs in step 2. Cut the rebar piece to fit this opening and weld it in place inside the body. Repeat for another brace near the back of the body.

12 Weld the neck in place. (You may want to dry fit the neck to achieve the desired angle. You may even have to use the cutting torch to cut the neck on the ends in order to accomplish this.)

13 Put the head made from the blade guard onto the neck. Position it to suit you and weld it into place. (Use the welder to tack it in place beforehand if you wish, so you can step back and check its position before you weld permanently.)

14 Make the eyes out of the two hex nuts on either side of the head. Hold them down in place with the pliers while you tack them down, then weld them on.

15 Now it's time to finish up with the toes and spur, which you'll weld onto the leg that extends into the ground. Take the two $3^1/2$ inch (8.9 cm) long pieces of $^1/2$-inch (1.3 cm) rebar (from step 2) and weld them in the shape of a "V" in the front of the bend at the bottom of the leg Weld the remaining straight piece directly behind the "V."

16 The flamingo is finished! Leave the bird in its natural weathered state, preserve it with a rust preventive spray, or paint it. Keep an eye on it because all your neighbors will want to move it to their own yards!

Bugs from old tool parts: praying mantis, ladybug, and centipede

Elephant with trunk made from a potbelly stove leg

Yard guard from car parts

ALL DESIGNS BY JIMMY HOPKINS

Salvaged spikes and railroad yard parts pop up in the garden as sturdy flowers.
DESIGN BY MARILYN DRABICKI & LARRY FREER

Iron Tuteur with Iron Ball, constructed from salvaged metal pieces and wire.
DESIGN AND PHOTO BY BRAD OLIVER

A corrugated metal elephant takes a nap in the garden.
PHOTO BY G. MICHAEL SHOUP, ANTIQUE ROSE EMPORIUM

Harold, constructed from nineteenth-century farm tools.
DESIGN AND PHOTO BY CHRISTOPHER SITTIG

Bird Feeder Beacon, constructed from harrow disks and machine parts.
DESIGN AND PHOTO BY JAMES CHRISTOPHER SITTIG